VISION
BUILDING

Knowing Where You're Going
Peter Brierley

All royalties from this book will go
towards the costs of further research for the church

CHRISTIAN RESEARCH

LONDON

British Library Cataloguing in Publication Data

Brierley, Peter, 1938—
  Vision building.
  1. Great Britain. Christian church
  I. Title
  274.1

  ISBN 0-340-51388 8 Pbk

First published in Great Britain by Hodder and Stoughton 1989
Reprinted, with permission, by Christian Research 1994

Published by Christian Research
Vision Building, 4 Footscray Road, Eltham,
London SE9 2TZ

Printing and production by Nuprint Ltd,
Station Road, Harpenden, Herts AL5 4SE

To my mother and late father whose vision for life has been deeply embedded within.

Also to James Tysoe, David Cormack and Peter Holmes, who respectively taught me the art, science and practice of vision building.

Be Thou my Vision, O Lord of my heart;
Naught be all else to me, save that Thou art –
Thou my best thought, by day or by night,
Waking or sleeping, Thy presence my light.

High King of heaven, after victory won,
May I reach heav'n's joys, O bright heaven's Sun!
Heart of my own heart, whatever befall,
Still be my Vision, O Ruler of all.

Ancient Irish Hymn

ACKNOWLEDGMENTS

Many people have helped me with this book, though often unconsciously – the word spoken, the suggestion made, the conclusions drawn from a meeting, or the words written in many books. Especially, I would thank those who have participated in MARC Europe's Vision Workshops, who have given me so much more than I ever gave them. To all such personal and impersonal encounters, my very grateful thanks.

I record too, my tremendous appreciation and support to Jenny Rogers who edited the first lengthy version of this book reducing it to manageable size and encouraging me all the time to keep going. Without her help it probably would not have got here. How she squeezed it into her full schedule, I do not know, but it was a great privilege to have her expert hand, though I take full responsibility for errors and imperfections.

I am most grateful too to Dee Frankling especially and Lois Pratt who patiently and willingly took on the seemingly endless burden of typing and amending the manuscript.

Thank you each one for all your help.

CONTENTS

1 Visions – What for *me*?   11
2 The Context of Vision   39
3 Vision and the Scriptures   81
4 Finding your Vision   107
5 Getting a Corporate Vision   135
6 Assimilating the Vision   173
7 Running with the Vision   197
Notes   203
Index   211
Scripture Index   219

LIST OF TABLES

1. Total UK Church members.   49
2. Adult Church life in England, Wales and
   Scotland.   51
3. Attendance by sex in 1980 and 1990.   53
4. Change in Christian affiliation by generation. 64
5. Change in Christian affiliation in a lifetime. 65
6. Size of churches.   66
7. Number of ministers.   68
8. Age of ministers.   69
9. Total money given to Christian organisations.   72
10. Total money given to Christian organisations
    compared with the number of organisations.   73
11. Total money given to Christian organisations
    by Church members.   74
12. Protestant missionaries 1972–2000.   77
13. Catholic missionaries 1982–1994.   78

LIST OF DIAGRAMS

1. Membership change in British churches.   50
2. Religious structure of population.   62
3. The changing religious community in the UK.   63
4. Income given to Christian organisations against cost-of-living.   72
5. Income per organisation against cost-of-living.   73
6. Giving per Church member and average earnings.   75
7. Table of gifts.   116
8. Table of skills.   118
9. Church membership of an Anglican church.   139
10. The ministries of a church.   147
11. Example of a 'footprint'.   151
12. Planning the vision.   167
13. Planning the vision this year.   168
14. Keeping the vision central.   169
15. Planning the vision each year.   170
16. Development of the vision.   171
17. A structure for vision.   176
18. The Christian Maslow hierarchy.   187
19. Anticipated income over the next decade.   192

PREFACE TO SECOND PRINTING

I am naturally delighted that this book should be found worth reprinting. Although it was originally published by Hodder & Stoughton (now Hodder Headline), they have kindly agreed that we may use their setting for this reprint, thus making it financially possible. The cover is however new to this reprint.

There have been many positive reactions to the book, for which we are most grateful. The desire behind the book is simply to help leaders, especially of churches and Christian organisations, to move forward creatively into the future. We trust it will continue to do that.

The book has not been updated, though a few misprints in the original have been corrected. It was deemed simplest and best, as well as cheapest, to do it that way. It means that we have been able to pass on some of the savings to the reader – this edition is cheaper than the first, despite it appearing five years later! Those who would like an update of the figures in Chapter 2 are invited to write to the author at Christian Research (the address is on the back of the title page).

It is intended to continue to use the book for 'Vision Workshops' — applications of the principles to individual people, churches or organisations — and for seminars on the subject. Details of both can be readily obtained by writing to Christian Research, the successor body to MARC Europe, although a separately and independently registered charity. Christian Research has followed MARC Europe's vision by desiring that 'the use of research for strategic planning for growth will be commonplace by the year 2000'. In that way may our slogan be fulfilled: Turning data into decisions.

Peter Brierley, August 1994

1: VISIONS – what for *me*?

It started like so many evenings. Mum and Dad at home and Jimmy playing after tea. Mum and Dad were absorbed with jobs and did not notice the time. It was a full moon and some of the light seeped through the windows. Then Mum glanced at the clock. 'Jimmy, it's time for you to go to bed. Go up now and I'll come and settle you later.'

Like most five-year olds, Jimmy was not keen to go to bed, but this evening he was dutifully obedient and went upstairs. An hour or so later his mother came up to check all was well, and to her astonishment found that her son was staring quietly out of his window at the moonlit scenery.

'What are you doing, Jimmy?'

'I'm looking at the moon, Mummy.'

'Well, it's time to go to bed now, darling.'

As one reluctant boy settled down, he said, 'Mummy, you know one day I'm going to walk on the moon.'

Who could have known that the boy in whom the dream was planted that night, would survive a near fatal motorbike crash which broke almost every bone in his body, and would bring it to fruition thirty-two years later when James Irwin stepped on to the moon's surface, just one of the twelve representatives of the human race to have done so?

The Major felt a deep responsibility for his country. The turmoil of war which plagued the Indo-China territories in the 1960s and early 1970s made life fraught with difficulties. Not least so for Major Chirrac Taing in the Cambodian army. When he was converted to Christ his earnest desire was to see his fellow countrymen won for the Lord. Yet he was not blind to career opportunities and so accepted the invitation to study for a degree in Edinburgh, arriving in Britain in 1972 with his wife and child.

Meanwhile the American offensives in Vietnam had become more and more bogged down and eventually the United States left Saigon one sorry day in February 1975. The closure of their Embassy in Cambodia followed shortly afterwards and almost immediately the Pol Pot Khmer Rouge regime began. Major Taing had felt compelled to go back to help the Church in his native homeland in their hour of need in 1973, planning for his family to join him later. This never became possible and he was last seen giving out tracts in April 1975, being almost certainly killed by the nonsensical brutality of those who caused the deaths of perhaps two million Cambodian people.

But the vision he had left behind was clear. An organisation called Southeast Asia Outreach (SAO) began refugee work in the many camps on the Laos border among the Hmong speaking people who had fled there from their native Cambodia.

Mark Timmins never knew Major Chirrac. He left Birmingham to be a missionary in Thailand with his wife Angela and two boys to work with SAO, in the mid 1980s. He yearned to start a church among those settlers in Thailand who spoke Hmong. In 1985 it began and on home leave in 1988 he was able to describe how the Lord had built a church of nearly thirty people.

'My dream,' he quietly continued, 'is to see a whole series of churches in border towns so that when opportunity allows people will be ready to plant the Gospel seed again in Cambodian soil.'

One man's vision in the process of being fulfilled by another.

They could never have dreamt the outcome. Initially all they were conscious of was the needs of their own city. Years of social neglect, loose morals and spiritual darkness drove them to prayer. Who could change their city? God could. How might God change their town? Through sending revival. How to get revival? By prayer.

So it was in 1934 that a group of men took a day off from work – itself an indication of their earnestness. The loss of one-sixth of a week's wage was a considerable sacrifice. And they prayed in the North Carolina town of Charlotte for spiritual revival in their city.

As so often happens when we pray in earnest, God extended their vision. They found themselves praying not just for Charlotte but for the whole of the state of North Carolina, then for the whole of America. And then they prayed, 'God do something in this city that will touch the entire world.'

He answered their prayer but they did not realise it for many years. Nothing appeared to happen, except later that year the sixteen-year old son of one of those praying men was converted. The son's name was Billy Graham.

Dr Graham has touched the world. He has had the privilege of preaching to more men about Christ than any one man who has yet lived. He has visited virtually every country in the world and his books, films, and radio programmes have touched many more. He has also stimulated over the last twenty years a series of congresses looking at the whole subject of *world* evangelisation. The most significant of these held in Lausanne, Switzerland in July 1974, brought together over 4,000 church leaders, produced a far-reaching Lausanne Covenant, and perpetuated the 'vision of the wholeness of the Gospel in a world of contrasts.'[1] A second, equally significant, was held in Manila in July 1989, and produced the Manila Manifesto, which supplemented the Covenant.

THE NEED FOR VISION

Men and women have always been driven by hopes, dreams and visions of what might be. Telford dreamed of a waterway system covering Britain, and his magnificent canal routes are still enjoyed and used two centuries later. Brunel conceived of a metal ship, and the first iron steam ship, *SS Great Britain*, was built in Bristol nearly 140 years ago. So what do visions do for us?

Visions stimulate

Father Elias Chacour is a remarkable man. He lives in the Galilean village of Ibillin, and is responsible for a secondary school for Israeli Arabs. He draws from the whole of Galilee and seeks to provide a school of the highest academic level as well as vocational training to a standard unmatched elsewhere. His reason is simply because he knows 'the only hope for the next generation of Palestinians is to be able to take on the Israelis at their own level of skill', by which he means skills of peace not war. 'We cannot,' he says to visitors, 'get by any more on history and poetry.' So he builds his school as finance allows and dedicates his life to the fulfilment of his dream. It is not just the work he is doing that is important. It is the way in which he is doing it that stimulates others.

Visions transform

Lee Iacocca is a giant in the motor industry. After forty years of experience he had a clear understanding of what was needed when he was appointed President of the Chrysler Corporation. He could see the many weaknesses in their product line, management structure and financial control, and set about changing them. His perceptive and articulate diagnosis of the situation meant that his hearers felt compelled to follow his vision for the future. He challenged the organisation to its core, but his solution was credible. He expressed his convictions so that the values and needs of the work-force were integrated with his desire for an efficient and responsive auto industry. He brought Chrysler from twenty years of decline through to massive recovery in profit and market share.[2] The person – man or woman – is the key for transformation. And the time – the 'chairos' time as some call the Greek word meaning opportunity – must be right. In God's hands these so often come together.

Visions drive

William Tyndale's vision was that the English people should have the Scriptures in their own language. Only Latin Scriptures were allowed in his day because the apparent threat from the Lollards led the Church to ban English translations of the Bible in 1408. Tyndale sought the help of the moderate Bishop of London, Cuthbert Tunstall, but received no help as Tunstall was determined to resist Lutheranism in Britain and saw the Bible in English as a threat. Tyndale realised he would get no help in England so he sailed for Germany in 1524. He said on one occasion to an antagonistic clergyman, 'if God spares my life, ere many years pass, I will cause a boy that driveth the plough shall know more of the Scriptures than thou dost.'[3] Three years after Tyndale's betrayal and execution in 1536, Henry VIII ordered every church in England to have a copy of the Scriptures. The fruit of Tyndale's driving vision lasted centuries and made Britain 'the people of the book'.

John Sung returned to his native China in 1929 armed with an American doctorate degree. His father was glad as it meant he could now help provide for the education of his six brothers. But, unusually for a Chinese, he disobeyed the command of his Christian father. John Sung said he felt that God was telling him to evangelise China and South-East Asia instead. He had a vision of people following Christ and felt he had just fifteen years to fulfil it. Over that period, committed to the fulfilment of his vision, he drove himself to do the work of a dozen men. Asia and the South Pacific today owe a tremendous debt to his ministry. He died in 1944.[4]

Visions are essential

What, for me? Yes, for you. For my church? Yes, for your church. For my organisation? Yes, for your organisation. The most frequently used Scripture in this connection is, 'Where there is no vision, the people perish.' (Proverbs 29:18 AV) Where there is no vision, society perishes. Where there is no vision the church perishes. Where there is no vision the para-church agency perishes. Where there is no vision, the leaders perish. Where there is no vision, you and I perish. You need to have a vision, a sense of where you are going and how you might get there. How we get a vision, or get back our vision, is what this book is all about. A recent business report on the electronic industry in Britain said it was rapidly losing out to foreign competition. Why? 'It lacked visionary leadership.'[5] Albert Einstein once wrote, 'Imagination is more important than knowledge.'

All Souls Church has a strategic ministry in Regent Street next to the BBC headquarters. Its John Nash building is in need of repair from London's acid-ridden grime and soot. So the Revd Richard Bewes launched an appeal for three-quarters of a million pounds to restore it. His powerfully articulated vision for a church physically fit to cope with the spiritual needs of the thousands who live and work nearby was essential for the church's restoration.

Visions are scriptural

The Bible is full of people who followed their vision successfully. Moses in the wilderness, surrounded by perhaps two million ex-slaves, having spent forty days on Mount Sinai receiving the Ten Commandments, feeling God's miraculous power work through him on a dozen occasions, still prayed, 'I pray thee, show me thy glory.' He knew his task – to take the Israelites back to the Promised Land – but he yearned for that deeper calling. God heard Moses, and graciously answered him. That sight enabled Moses to keep on going for forty more years, for he 'endured, as seeing Him who is invisible', as Hebrews 11:27 (AV) tells us.

The ordinary person may not feel such a deep need to know God's glory. Yet every Christian wants to do God's will. 'Teach me, O Lord, to follow your decrees' is the cry of the Psalmist (Psalm 119:33, NIV) and many others who want to walk in God's truth and to fear His name.

Troubled people yearn to know God's understanding. A friend of mine lost her husband suddenly through cancer of the liver after seventeen years of marriage. Why did He take him? The question cannot be directly answered, but indirectly she affirms, 'because he had done all that the Lord wanted him to'. Job wanted to argue with the Almighty, because he could not understand how God could take away his family, his livelihood, his house, and his reputation. But though God might slay him, Job would still trust him, for he knew that his Redeemer lived. Centuries later, Martin Luther would exclaim, 'Here I stand, I can do no other'.

Uncertain disciples wanted a vision of the future. So many changes seemed about to take place. The opposition was mounting, the political storm growing. The denunciations of Jesus had become more explicit – 'woe to you, scribes and Pharisees, hypocrites'. His prophecies of destruction seemed total, 'there will not be left here one stone upon another, that will not be thrown down'. So the disciples came to the Master and asked Him, 'What will be the sign of your coming and of the close of the age?' Jesus described the future in practical terms of what to look out for (the desecration of the holy place), what to pray for (it may not be in winter or on a Sabbath), what not to believe ('Lo, here is the Christ!'), and indicated that the Son of Man would come 'as lightning comes'[6] – suddenly, brilliantly, undeniably, visibly, unexpectedly, dangerously. You cannot know when the lightning will flash; keep on going till it comes. So today both mature and new Christians search and pray for the Lord's understanding of what they must do, what their vision might be.

Visions are contemporary

In a unique experiment in July 1988, Mikhail Gorbachev allowed a BBC broadcast in Russia in which Margaret Thatcher answered questions by phone-in. At one stage she drew a comparison between herself and Mr Gorbachev: 'I have met politicians the world over and I recognise someone who is bold and courageous when I see them and I recognise someone with vision for the future, and who believes in it so strongly that they go on and on until their goal is obtained. In a way I felt like that when I became Prime Minister.'[7]

Speaking at a Labour Party Conference in Chesterfield,

Neil Kinnock said, 'We have to choose between striving for a dream or only being a dreamer. Let us follow a vision for the future rather than a mirage of the past.'[8]

At the final service in Canterbury Cathedral of the Twelfth Lambeth Conference, the Rt Revd Edmond Browning said, 'the Anglican church must not become a museum of the past, but a household of vision for the future. Authority is found in transformation not stagnation.'[9]

By the turn of the century, well over half the world's population will live in the great urban centres of the world. 'To reach them for Christ will require Christians who have discovered God's plan for their own lives, within His plan for the World,' Billy Graham said, and continued, 'my vision is to see Christians, who are spiritually equipped, move out of the pews and into action where they live and work. That's why we are developing the Billy Graham Training Center at The Cove. I believe that it's imperative for the laity to have a thorough and workable understanding of God's word.' So, in Asheville, North Carolina, a beautifully wooded property is being provided with facilities to enable such vital training to take place.[10]

Visions face the future

When, as Vice-President, George Bush chose Senator Dan Quayle as his running mate for the Presidential election, he explained that he was going for 'a man of the future, a young man born in the middle of this century and in the middle of America.'[11] He was chosen because he would be going into the next century – a man with a future.

Much discontent surfaced in British school life in 1986 with many teachers' strikes. Sir Keith Joseph had 'failed to produce a vision for education capable of exciting the public imagination' despite making many efforts to do so.[12] It was clear that parents, local government, central government and teachers were all blaming each other. Mr Kenneth Baker was then made Secretary of State for Education, and building on Sir Keith's work, has provided a vision for the future, not agreed with by all, but in the process of being followed through with determination and a radical Education Act in which the various groups involved will have to interact more specifically. How successful it will be remains to be seen.

Part of our responsibility as God's stewards is to have a concern for the future. The Old Testament refers to our 'children's children' and 'the third and fourth generation of those who love me'. This future orientation becomes in the New Testament the future of the new order in Christ, the Kingdom. The West German theologian Dorothy Sölle has said that 'to be human is to have an elemental relation to the future'. The details of the future are in the hands of the Lord, but you and I must not act indifferently towards the future, for we are stewards, and have a responsibility towards the future. He who has the world in His hands has our world in His hands too – our persons, our times, our gifts, our resources.

The future requires plans. Robert Schuller once wrote, 'If we do not plan for the future, we plan for no future.'[13] The churches in Britain need strategic vision to plan forward three, five, or ten years. 'But it is God's visions we must fit in with – not ours,' urges Bishop Michael Baughen.[14] 'It is God's will for *our* church that is important. To copy the blueprint of somewhere else can mean disaster. Every church must face their own unique opportunities. How God blesses one church may not be His will for others.'

The need for vision is paramount. Visions can stimulate, transform, drive us. They are essential, scriptural and contemporary. They face the future. I believe that visions are, as it were, etched on our hearts by the Lord. That vision has to be drawn out of our hearts to bring it to an emotional, intellectual, spiritual intensity, so that we not only hear the voice of God saying, 'This is the way, walk in it', but in response we also commit ourselves to follow. The vision is often based on our concerns. With Abram we cry, 'I have no children'; with Moses, 'You can't kill your people'; with Samson, 'Let me die with the Philistines'; with David, 'God's covenant box kept in a tent!' What, then, is vision?

DEFINING VISION

'Vision is the art of seeing things invisible' wrote the Anglo-Irish seventeenth century satirist Jonathan Swift. In one sense he is correct. Moses so endured; David 'always saw the Lord before' him; Paul instructs us to set our 'minds on the things that are above'. Amy Carmichael, the founder of the Dohnavur Fellowship in South India wrote to one of the children she looked after, 'work for the Invisible all the time'.[15] Bill Grant is a Yeti hunter in the mountains of Tibet, and during a BBC interview before setting off on his latest expedition said, 'only those who see the invisible can do the impossible'. Whilst vision relates to the invisible, it has to be more concrete than that.

The will, the word and the work of God

God is sovereign. He is over all. Nothing happens without His acquiescence, though He is not the cause of evil, nor the originator of temptation. He is the Creator; He formed the earth initially; He will remake it again. The Word is the Son of God who came to redeem the world and by His death to enable salvation to be preached to all. The Word made flesh has by His Spirit breathed into the Word making the Holy Scriptures readable, written for our learning, discipline and training. The Work of God is carried out today through the Holy Spirit who convinces the world of sin, righteousness and judgment, and who dwells within every believer allowing the grace, truth and love of Jesus to flourish. The Will, Word and Work of God thus reflect the Trinity of God the Father, God the Son and God the Spirit, whose key purpose is to further the Kingdom of God. Such overriding control and sovereignty is above all our searchings for vision, and desires for service.

Purpose

Why is your church here? What is the reason for your organisation's existence? Ray Anderson put it like this:

'While each Christian organisation has a discrete purpose and mission of its own, it does not have a will of its own. Rather, these organisations exist to fulfil God's purpose in the world and to embody this Will in their own purposes and actions.'[16]

Here are examples of organisational purpose statements which indicate their essential *raison d'être*:

Crusaders: Reaching today's young people for Christ; preparing them for responsible Christian living and developing their gifts of leadership for tomorrow's world.

British Institute of Management: To promote the development and the successful exercise of management skills.

Bible Society: To glorify God by increasing the number of people who own, use, value and share the Bible with others, throughout the world.

Mothers' Union: To be specially concerned with all that strengthens and preserves marriage and Christian family life.

Churches likewise can have purpose statements. Here are three taken from the *Tyne and Wear Christian Directory*:[17]

Christ Church, Gateshead: Anglican presence in the inner city.

St Agnes, Roman Catholic Church, Gateshead: Serving the spiritual needs of the parishioners in Crawcrook and surrounding areas.

Whitburn Methodist, South Tyneside: A village chapel forming a nucleus for wider sharing.

Mission

Mission is subordinate to purpose and relates to the here-and-now environment. Mission answers the question 'How?' and is sometimes taken as the key objective of an organisation or church. Two organisations may have a similar purpose but different missions. Thus Oxfam and Christian Aid both have as their purpose the alleviation of suffering through relief and development worldwide. But Oxfam deals with this in a participative manner (by organising actions at local level bringing in extra staff and resources as necessary directly), whereas Christian Aid handles their work in a mostly nonparticipative manner – by providing resources (usually finance) to organisations already in a position in a country to handle the needs. One single organisation may have two distinct missions, like the Salvation Army with both a Church and a Social mission. Such work can helpfully be reflected in a statement, like the following:

MARC Europe: Enabling Christian leaders throughout Western Europe to use their resources more effectively for evangelism and growth.

Salesian Sisters: Renewed Christ-centred communities reaching out to the young with creative daring in the spirit of the founder and involving the rest of the Salesian family.

Churches may have a similar purpose – to preach the Gospel. But this could be handled differently by an inner city church, a council estate church or a rural church. One may concentrate on social or physical needs, another on families, another focus on the provision of fellowship for all age groups. Examples of similar church mission statements are:

Ebenezer Church, South Tyneside (Brethren): Providing regular family worship, Bible-based teaching and preaching of the Gospel.

John Knox United Reformed Church, Newcastle: Flexible worship patterns, and working to meet the social and spiritual needs of the community.

The relationship between the Will of God, Purpose and Mission may be depicted thus:

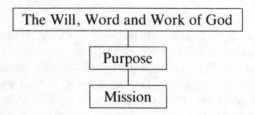

Vision

Vision follows purpose and mission. The purpose of a church or organisation changes very rarely if at all – perhaps once a

century. The mission of a church or organisation will probably change more frequently than once a century, but still not
very often – once in a generation perhaps. The vision however
is more short-lived, although still relatively long-term with
respect to the present. It might be for five, ten or perhaps
twenty years. The vision thus seeks to answer the questions
'What?' and 'When?' What do you hope to achieve, and by
what date? Vision is therefore much more specifically time-
related. In the context of this book, the word is thus being
used as 'long-term planning'. Such usage is becoming common, but for the Christian, it is, in many ways, a more
emotive and inspirational word.

A vision statement therefore needs to embody a date,
either implicitly or explicitly. MARC Europe's vision for
example does it explicitly. It is 'that by the year 2000, strategic thinking will be commonplace amongst Christian leaders
in Europe'. (The phrase 'strategic thinking' is then further
defined.)

Many organisations will have several visions. The Salesian
Sisters for example have four challenging sentences:

1) To inspire others with the joyful warmth of Christian
   love, respect, values and understanding in a family
   relationship.
2) To allow others to capture responsible, caring, challenging and enthusiastic leadership roles.
3) To encourage young people to commit themselves to
   Christ, as Catholics, through service, the Word and the
   Church.
4) To renew ourselves in the areas of prayer, joyful enthusiasm, challenge and courage so that we are signs of
   hope to young people and the world.

The visions of Southeast Asian Outreach numbered five
when their Council met to agree them in March 1987. By the
year 2000 their aims were to have:

1) Strengthened the Church in Cambodia.
2) Established churches equipped to evangelise the
   peoples of South-East Asia.
3) Established a continuing service for the churches of the
   dispersed peoples of South-East Asia world-wide.

4) Trained cross-cultural Christian workers to serve all nations.
5) Established a network of churches supporting SAO and its objectives.

Such examples do not only relate to para-church agencies. Churches also may have visions. Here are examples of some:

Above Bar Church, Southampton: To encourage every believing member of the congregation to be a maturing and witnessing Christian, believing that in this way God may be pleased to double the number of believers connected with Above Bar Church in the next ten years.

Brandhall Church, Warley: To reach the area so that a caring, teaching, counselling, serving Church be formed, who will evangelise and stand for God in the local Church and world-wide communities.

What comes after vision?

A vision demands that things will be different. To begin translating the vision into action, it is useful to break it up into between three and six 'thrusts' or 'directions'. World Vision for example has six:

1) Ministering to children and families.
2) Providing emergency aid.
3) Developing self-reliance.
4) Reaching the unreached.
5) Leadership enhancement.
6) Mission challenge.

Campus Crusade for Christ has five:

1) Outreach to strategic groups.
2) Training world-wide.
3) Prayer support groups.
4) Recruitment of workers.
5) Effective funding mechanism.

The Mothers' Union also has five:

1) Teaching about marriage.
2) Encouraging parents.
3) World-wide prayer.
4) Promoting a secure society.
5) Helping those in adversity.

In the 1987 'Keep Sunday Special' campaign spearheaded by the Jubilee Centre in Cambridge, the major thrust was simple – 'towards church members and the man in the street, and through them to local MPs'.

Goals, priorities, plans, actions

These are included here for the sake of completeness but will not be developed at length as there are many books on time management. Dr David Cormack's excellent book *Seconds Away!* – fifteen rounds in the effective use of time – is especially recommended.[18] Many courses on this subject are also available, such as those put on by Time Management International or from a specifically Christian perspective, MARC Europe's *The Effective Use of Time*.

Goals are specific measurable targets. Time-related goals are set for a shorter period than a vision statement.

Drawing up a list of priorities will help you decide which task to tackle first. Which things are of greater urgency, lesser urgency for you? Which are of greater value, lesser value?

Once goals and priorities are established, plans need to be developed. How will we actually accomplish what we've set out to do? There are many techniques for planning and a number are helpfully listed in Ed Dayton and Ted Engstrom's book *Strategy for Leadership*.[19] However you do it, a list of what you intend to do is essential, together with a time reference or a chart with target dates. 'Vision building is not dealing with future decisions,' says Peter Drucker, the guru of modern management thinking, 'but with the futurity of present decisions.' Dr John R. Mott, the visionary leader who, a hundred years ago, coined the phrase 'Evangelise the world in this generation' once said, 'The end of the planning is the beginning of the doing.'

Putting it all together

The order of all these items is important. Action is essential, but it comes after vision. All the above elements can be framed in a single sequence, thus:

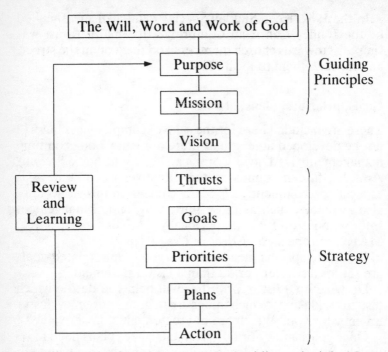

By listing the first three terms as 'guiding principles' I am suggesting the relative immovability of the essential reasons for the existence of your church or organisation. In practice these would be articulated by reference to the Bible, the Constitution or Rules, Articles or Memorandum of Association, Principles and Practice or other similar documents. These guidelines might be changed in detail from time to time, but only rarely in their essential nature.

You must build in opportunities for:

1) *Reviewing and learning*. Creating a vision is a long term process, and you will need some way of regularly reviewing the overall progress.

2) *Strategy*. This is the mechanics of vision, and includes all the features necessary to achieve the vision – thrusts, goals, priorities, plans, review mechanisms and so on. A strategy is a means to an end and is associated with:

   1) The end – the vision – the position to be achieved

   2) A time scale

3) Goals or targets to be achieved along the way
4) Priorities – those things to be tackled first
5) Performance criteria – the standards required
6) Review

Is all this spiritual?

The Bible Society puts it well. 'The Society seeks to accomplish its purpose under the guidance of the Holy Spirit, using the best professional management methods consistent with biblical standards. We try to work within a biblical framework of priorities that puts our commitment to God first and people second and with a bias towards using our resources to help people in disadvantaged parts of the world.'[20]

Many biblical examples support these processes. Nehemiah went to Jerusalem with a clear purpose – to build its wall. His mission was to do it uniting the community. His vision was to complete the wall to defensive height in the least time possible. His thrusts were based on building, defence, resourcing and encouraging the work-force. His goals were broken up into finite sections of the wall at which each family group worked. His priorities changed when it was necessary to provide for defence but his key priority for keeping going with the wall building never faltered. His plans were based on a private, personal and comprehensive inspection one moon-lit night.

Paul's purpose was to take the Gospel to the Gentiles. His mission was to plant churches in various towns of the Roman Empire by preaching the word first to the Jews and then to the Gentiles. His vision was to found a church in each town that would begin the evangelisation of that town and its surrounding rural area. His thrusts were journeys, letter writing, church support and encouragement. His goals were a functioning church wherever he went – which meant the appointment of suitable men as elders. His priorities were to move as the Spirit led, to go to the Jews first, and to preach the whole Gospel. His plans were fulfilled in three pioneering missionary journeys, and an unplanned voyage to Rome. His actions resulted in the spread of the church to all parts of the Roman

Empire, and the conversion of the Emperor within 300 years. Centuries later, as one of the millions who has benefited from the results of all his work, I'm personally very grateful he did it so well!

Yes, visions, plans and actions are scriptural. They reflect the heart of God and are seen in the outworking of His love for all the world.

CHARACTERISTICS OF VISION

Vision is the vital fulcrum which holds total strategy and guiding principles together. The one without the other is useless. Hence the need for a vision. What then are some of the features of a vision?

Visions are personal

Essentially, they relate to an individual. Virtually all the visions in the Scriptures come to a single person, though there are hints of corporate occasions, as with the angels appearing to the shepherds the night Jesus was born. The vision may come to be shared with a group, and followed maybe by hundreds (or in Moses' case, millions), but the prime mover is usually just one person.

Likewise for a church or organisation. The vision that moves it will primarily be that of the minister, senior pastor, general secretary, chief executive or whoever is officially recognised as the leader. While he or she is with that church or organisation the vision of the church or organisation will be essentially his or hers. Of course they will listen to others, frame the vision in the light of the perceived needs and opportunities, as realistically as they can in deferment to other people's wishes, but at the end of the day it is usually that one person's vision. It may be called the church's vision or organisation's vision, but that is essentially because the key individual personifies the church or organisation and is identified with it. Once the time comes for him or her to move on, the vision may change, and indeed will in any case need to be freshly thought out and articulated. Thus while we may write of forming the vision of a church or organisation, the crucial first step is identifying the individual's vision.

Visions are clear

A vision is known. It can be talked about. It is specific. You can relate to it. People know what it is you are hoping to do. Six years ago my brother's vision was 'to buy a narrowboat so that the children of Lewisham can have the opportunity of having a holiday and see the countryside'. Everyone knew what he meant. He achieved it with a lot of hard work.

Visions are shareable

A vision may come to an individual but it must be shared by others. The vision must be communicated. Others have to agree with it, and in agreeing, will follow it. Thus will the visionary leader be followed. John Naisbitt, the author of *Megatrends*, writes, 'Followers create leaders. Period.' For leaders to be followed, their vision must be shareable.

Visions are realistic

A vision will invariably build upon and use your gifts. Visions from God do not suddenly move a person in a broad new direction. God builds on our previous experience of walking with Him, and our past understanding of Him, and then He moves us on to new levels of revelation.

David Puttnam, the Director of the award winning film, *Chariots of Fire*, said on a radio programme, 'You can't just stare out of the window with your dream; you have to tailor your dreams to reality. I'm glad I worked in advertising, because that taught me realism.'

Brian Mawhinney, Under Secretary of State in Northern Ireland, speaking at the 1988 Chief Executive Officers' Conference said, 'Christians need wisdom to discern the right level of expectation. If it is too low we become apathetic; if too high we become frustrated; if it is just right, we have fulfilment. The world's perception of our vision and the Church's perception may not be the same. Hence Christians need to take a realistic view of their gifts, resources, opportunities and experience. They may not change the world in total, but may influence change in one part.'

Visions are beyond oneself

The new corporate mission statement of Canon Inc, the Japanese camera and photocopier maker states, 'We believe that private enterprise has a role above and beyond simply making a profit. In today's world, fragmented by political, economic, religious, cultural, and other borders, private enterprise has a special niche to fill. Private enterprise can reach beyond these divisions, provide a *world-wide perspective* on issues, and bring people together.'[21] They are looking beyond themselves. So must all vision makers.

We must move from a narrow, individualistic vision to, if necessary, a world-wide vision. 'For God so loved the *world* that He gave His one and only Son,' John (3:16, NIV) tells us. Michael Harper, founder of Sharing of Ministries Abroad, says 'to be real (the vision) must be global!'

Preaching at a European Christian service recently the Archbishop of Canterbury said, 'As we need local loyalties so we also need to look beyond them to a wider world and a different future. Vision is a confidence of the infinite possibilities for the people of God – it is a refusal to be locked into fatalism and despair. A preacher in our islands at the beginning of the last century cried out in one of his sermons: "If anyone says war is inevitable, disease is inevitable, poverty is inevitable, I shout out: thank God that's a lie; Jesus Christ lives and His Kingdom will come".'

Visions are energising

Where is our energy? Our spiritual energy comes from the Holy Spirit but it is possible for us to misuse it. Where our vision is, our energy will follow. John Haggai in his book *Lead On* gives twelve characteristics of leadership and spends a whole chapter on energy! The American poet, Ralph Waldo Emerson, once wrote, 'Nothing great was ever achieved without enthusiasm'. John Haggai would endorse this and go further. Nothing significant for God can ever be accomplished by a man or woman with a lackadaisical attitude.

Energy will motivate. Used correctly it will enhance your faith, deepen your commitment, and give you more power. How do you find that energy? By finding your vision. Vision relates to a mindset, an attitudinal set of values. Change that mindset. Alter the psychology. Amend the values, and the new vision will release unbounded energy.

Visions are humbling

Paul in Ephesians makes some astounding statements. God created Adam and Eve, and yet planned from eternity (3:11) the work of Christ, implying He knew His creatures would fall. However many generations between Adam and Eve and the last years of the twentieth century, fancy the Lord knowing the total genealogy so well that *before* the foundation of the world, He chose *us* in Christ (1:4). He knew me before I was born. But He knew before my great-great-great grandfather was born too! If that is not sufficient, He also knows what I shall do with my life, for 'we are His workmanship, created in Christ Jesus for good works, which God prepared beforehand, that we should walk in them' (2:10, RSV). God has prepared the details of our lives to enable us to reach the potential He desires, to follow His will, obey His commands, and rejoice in Him.

Such knowledge is 'too wonderful for me' (Job 42:3). God is working His purposes out as year succeeds to year, but He is doing this not just in the macro, but in the micro of my life, my destiny, and my actions. Any vision I may have God knows. Indeed God must have given it. So the visionary needs to be a humble follower of the Lord. 'All that I am, He made me, All that I have, He gave me', goes the chorus, 'And all that ever I hope to be, Jesus alone must do for me.'

CONSEQUENCES OF VISIONS

A former General Manager of the Abbey National Building
Society, Terry Murphy, tells the story of his father who was an
instrument fitter. He used to say, 'If a job is not good enough
to carry your name, it's not good enough.' My own father
frequently used to say, 'If a job's worth doing, it's worth doing
properly.' So it is with a vision. We need to become identified
with it, to own it, acknowledge it, appropriate it. It will
become part of our life, part as it were of the warp and woof of
our being. One of the consequences of having a vision is
having a commitment to it. What are some of the other
consequences?

We will be attempting the impossible

A vision statement looks to the future, and will stretch us to
do what we are not strong enough to do alone. We trust in
God for guidance, help, endurance and His Spirit to enpower
us. When Ralph Winter felt God calling him to start the
United States School for World Mission he was led to a
suitable campus site in Pasadena, one of the outlying parts of
Los Angeles. It contained all the facilities that were needed,
and had the potential for growth, but the price was $15
million. 'That's impossible,' his friends said. But he raised the
first down-payment, and has now received loans and gifts
virtually to complete the rest. He attempted the impossible –
and did it.

Lewis Carroll in *Through the Looking Glass* tackles this
problem. The White Queen is speaking to Alice.

'I can't believe that,' said Alice.

'Can't you?' the Queen said, in a pitying tone. 'Try again:
draw a long breath and shut your eyes.'

Alice laughed: 'There's no use trying,' she said, 'one *can't*
believe impossible things.'

'I daresay you haven't had much practice,' said the Queen.
'When I was your age, I always did it for half-an-hour a day.
Why, sometimes I've believed as many as six impossible
things before breakfast.'

Most of us follow Alice – we don't believe in the impossible. The disciples felt that it was impossible for Jesus to have risen from the dead on the third day. No one had ever done that before. Who would believe in blue snow? But that's what the scientists found on Jupiter's moon Io as Voyager, the spacecraft, took coloured photographs as it swept past – a kind of volcanic precipitate.

The seven last words of the church are said to be, 'We have always done it this way.' Change? Impossible! But we follow an impossible God who can give us a vision to do the impossible.

We will be taking a risk

Every visionary takes a risk. If you don't take risks, you won't be an influence upon the world. You can analyse your position, determine your strengths and weaknesses, your opportunities and tasks, but you cannot predict where all the threats will come from. When Luis Palau held his Mission to London in 1984, the Queen's Park Rangers Football Stadium was hired for the meetings. The campaign was publicised to last just four weeks but the Executive Committee knew that the QPR authorities would allow them an extension if they wished. The first week of the Mission went well – dare they extend it? What of the costs? Would the people come? Would all the authorities be happy? They prayed, they asked, they consulted. And they decided to take the plunge and extend the Mission by two further weeks. The appropriate permissions were given. And the response? 43,000 people came on average every week for the first four weeks, and the extra last two weeks saw 82,000 people come altogether – virtually the same weekly attendance as the first month.[22] The Mission maintained its momentum, and did not crumble as some anticipated.

We will be exercising our faith

The French novelist and dramatist, André Gide once wrote, 'One doesn't discover new lands without consenting to lose sight of the shore for a very long time.' When Christopher Columbus sailed in his *Santa Maria* to search for a passage to the East Indies by sailing west, he went hoping to discover something new. He did – but not what he expected. Fancy finding a whole continent over there! Essentially he sailed in faith, and so must we in terms of our vision.

Our faith may come in different sizes. You may not be called to emulate George Müller who built five orphanage homes in Bristol towards the end of the nineteenth century without asking anyone for a single penny. Nor may you have the opportunity to develop an organisation like the China Inland Mission as Hudson Taylor did in the 1860s initially with just twenty-four missionaries, who worked in China without drawing any income.

Most of us have a much smaller faith. Like the disciples left at the foot of the Mount of Transfiguration the epileptic boy seems incurable. But we are called to have faith in Christ. 'Truly, I say to you,' He said on that occasion, 'if you have faith as a grain of mustard seed, you will say to this mountain, "Move hence to yonder place," and it will move; and nothing will be impossible to you' (Matthew 17:20, RSV).

The Christian life is a walk of faith. Our vision is a statement of faith. The famous faith chapter, Hebrews 11, begins 'Faith is the assurance of things hoped for, the conviction of things not seen' (RSV). Our vision is something we hope for, invisible, intangible, impossible. But we believe that through God it can be brought about.

Bob Dunnett, Vice-Principal of Birmingham Bible Institute, put it this way, 'Vision is that pulsating of heart which believes in what we know and pursues eagerly its fulfilment. Vision involves faith.'[23]

We will dream dreams

Martin Luther King's famous Washington speech concluded:

> And so today I still have a dream.
> I have a dream that one day men will rise up and come to
> see that they are made to live together as brothers.

I still have a dream this morning that one day every Negro in this country, every coloured person in the world, will be judged on the basis of the content of his character rather than the colour of his skin, and every man will respect the dignity and worth of human personality.

Our dreams are very precious to us. They were to Martin Luther King. They were to Joseph of old, even if he couldn't really understand them. Managers talk about goals, politicians about manifestos, army generals about strategies. Let church people talk of their *dreams*, their visions. Dreams have the power to motivate, challenge. They disturb us, they move us. They are intangible but compulsive. Visions emerge from our dreams.

Dreams are enduring. When Joseph's brothers scornfully said to themselves, 'Here comes this dreamer', they were outworking their previous decision not to try and understand what his dreams meant. They didn't like the sound of the dream and so sought to eliminate it by eliminating the dreamer. God stepped in through his brother Reuben, and Joseph was sold as a slave to the Egyptians. His dreams were not eliminated, and twenty or so years later were vindicated and fulfilled. His brothers eventually owed their lives to him. There are many dreamers in every church congregation. Let us pursue them: their dreams will enliven us.

We will face opposition

There is a price to pay for dreaming. Joseph spent many years in prison. Martin Luther King met an assassin's bullet. But American history over the last twenty years has shown that the death of the dreamer is not the death of the dream.

You are perhaps unlikely to encounter such drastic measures when you state your vision, but you might well find you generate negative attitudes. Others will be sceptical, disbelieving, disgruntled. They will probably criticise you for attempting the impossible.

Some people react to a vision by opting out – they are too busy to get involved further. But you need to be sure that is not an excuse hiding other feelings. Despite the pressures of short-term work, you also need to pursue long-term strategies and those who are so bound up with the present need to be released so they can contemplate the future. Building a bit of the future into one's present-day work may add to your 'busyness' but it will also help to fulfil your vision. As John Naisbitt states in *Megatrends*, 'Long-range plans must replace short-term profit or our decline will be steeper still'.

We will face the need to change

Change will be essential. Half the children in Britain leave school without any nationally recognised qualifications. Partly to combat that, twenty City Technology Colleges (CTCs) are being proposed. The newly appointed Chairman of the City Technology Colleges Trust Cyril Taylor, wrote, 'It is always a slow and difficult task to achieve change in education and realistically it will take some years for the CTCs to establish themselves. The need for a greatly increased skilled work-force is so vital, however, that the twenty CTCs should prove beacons of excellence from which other inner city schools can benefit.'[24] Our vision too may take years to get established.

The computer giant IBM is known world-wide. The corporation is founded on three basic business beliefs: respect for the individual, service to the customer and the pursuit of excellence. In 1914, the founder of IBM, Thomas J. Watson Snr said: 'We will change everything about our corporation. We will alter our terms and conditions, we will change our organisation and its products. We will change our policies. We will do whatever is necessary to keep our people challenged and motivated, to ensure that we have the money to invest in people, research and development, and to give our customers the best possible value. We will change everything except our beliefs.'[25] Likewise our vision may require us to change almost everything in our personal lives, our church or our organisation if it is to be fulfilled. That is how Lee Iacocca turned round Chrysler, and Sir Michael Edwardes British Leyland. It is maybe what God requires of us.

We will face dissatisfaction

Most will say with politician Reginald Maudling, 'We are all in favour of the future',[26] but in practice they are dissatisfied with your version of it. A vision creates followers, but not everyone in your church or organisation will necessarily wish to follow the vision of the leader. For those not so willing, it is better to change to another church or organisation. You will face dissatisfaction yourself. The vision is not being fulfilled fast enough. Or well enough. Maybe you do something wrong, but 'the man who makes no mistakes does not usually make anything'.[27] God often speaks to us in 'the broken places', as Tom Sine puts it.[28]

But dissatisfaction can be a powerful motivator. When Haggai wanted to move the returned Israelite exiles to re-build the temple of God, he tried to heighten their awareness of their discontent. The people had planted a harvest but it didn't produce enough. They had food, but not enough. They had refreshment, but never in the quantity they wanted. They had clothes, but still found themselves cold. They had money, but it seemed to go nowhere – like putting your wages 'into a bag with holes'.

Having achieved this understanding among the people, Haggai then pointed out what needed doing – rebuild the house of the Lord, so that He could appear in His glory. He reminded them of God's purposes for them: 'In this place I will give prosperity', and of God's power: 'My Spirit abides among you'.

But he didn't stop there. He was aware that the root of their dissatisfaction was the underlying political structures. So Haggai prophesied that the Lord was 'about to overthrow the throne of kingdoms . . . about to destroy the strength of the kingdom of the nations, and overthrow the chariots and their riders'. But the vision was clear – rebuild His House. Haggai used the people's dissatisfaction as a motivator for action, and then was able to promise an even deeper resolution for their ill-feeling.

Vision building is linked to tomorrow's world. But if there is to be a tomorrow for today's church or church organisation you have to focus that vision and put it into context.

2: THE CONTEXT OF VISION

To arrive at a vision you must know the relevant facts. The aim of this chapter is to give you a comparative framework for looking at your own church or organisation. If you are reading the book outside the United Kingdom then you will need to substitute data of your own.

If you find that your church attendance, or the donations to your organisation have grown 10% in the past year you will be pleased. But if you find that everyone else has grown 10% as well, you will just feel grateful you are 'normal'. If you find that everyone else has grown 15% you will wonder what is wrong with you! So a comparative framework is essential.

Problems of the data

Church data in this country are hard to come by:

Time series can be incomplete. Little consecutive information has been collected on the same basis for the last forty or fifty years.

There are timing differences. Church attendance if collected at all, is collected at different times. The Anglicans choose a Sunday in May, the Catholics the last Sunday in October. Such information is usually collected every year (though the Anglicans omitted 1975).

Different denominations have different definitions. Anglican church membership can be measured by those on the Electoral Roll, which is open to anyone over the age of sixteen attending a particular church, or living within its parish boundaries. Baptist church members are invariably those who have been baptised as adults by total immersion. Catholic church members are born of Catholic parents, and are usually baptised as infants. Some ethnic churches wish a potential church member to show the validity of his life in Christ over a period of at least six months.

Data are often not comprehensive. The Anglicans, Catholics, and Church of Scotland account for just over two-thirds of total church membership in these islands. But the remaining third is comprised of church members in over a hundred further different denominations, many of whom do not publish their figures.

Reactions of church people

Some feel collecting data is unscriptural. They recall David's punishment for attempting a population census in Israel. General Joab, David's commander-in-chief protested, but David overrode him with a direct order. And God punished him. But the reason was not the act of collecting data but David's pride because he wanted to know and perhaps boast about the large number of people he ruled. We are told the idea was prompted by Satan in 1 Chronicles 21. 'The numbering was a sin because it was self-glorification.'[1] Two censuses had been carried out before at God's specific request – before and after the Israelites' forty years in the wilderness – and the result? A book in the Bible called Numbers!

Some feel that the emphasis should be on quality not quantity. 'Not how many we are, but how holy we are.' It is right to guard against excessive dependence on one type of data – sheer quantity – but it is as wrong to swing totally to the opposite direction and look only on quality. Quantity statements are useful when the same thing is measured at a later time, as the trend gives valuable information. Whether something is growing or declining can be critical in determining our vision. After one presentation in which I had shown a number of graphs all going down, one church leader prayed, 'O God, move so that those graphs don't become true'. Quantitative information can stimulate our praying, encourage us in our work, and give us firm facts on which to move.

Some feel that data collection is unnecessary. If you belong to a small church that might be true, but many small churches grow, and there may come a time when everyone does not know everyone else. It is useful to know that you've grown from say 30 people in 1986 to 150 by 1988. If you've added 120 people in two years, will your present building or meeting place be big enough if a further 120 are added in the next two years? Collecting such simple information gives a realistic basis for planning for the future.

The value of statistics

But for all their weaknesses, any data are better than no data. You should not worry if the data are not as complete, as reliable or as comprehensive as you would wish. Take what you have and deduce what you can from it, even though of course you will always wish to aim for properly researched data whenever that is possible. Statistics can serve many useful purposes:

They allow trends to be evaluated. Where are we going? Such information may be uncomfortable – the Salvation Army dropped from 92,000 members in 1970 to 56,000 in 1987. But the Army's leaders used this information to work out strategies to change that situation, and have been teaching widely and following church growth methods in the last few years, so that the forecast for 1990 is 57,000 members. Not much growth? No, but a very great difference from the previous decline.

Information can stimulate thought. The saying that there are lies, damned lies and statistics is commonplace. It is easy to pour scorn on some facts, like the tale of the roadside merchant who was asked to explain how he could sell rabbit sandwiches so cheap. 'Well,' he explained, 'I have to put in some horsemeat too. But I mix them 50–50. One horse, one rabbit.' Professor Oliver Wendell Holmes, the American author who died in 1894, once wrote 'All fact-collectors, who have no aim beyond their facts, are one-storey men. Two-storey men compare, reason, generalise, using the labours of the fact-collectors as well as their own. Three-storey men idealise, imagine, predict; their best illumination comes from above, through the skylight.'[2] Christians may not feel too much of their illumination comes through the skylight, but will certainly agree that it comes from above!

They allow strategic action to be taken in critical areas. 'Renewing companies treat information as their main strategic advantage, and flexibility as their main strategic weapon. Their ability is to sense opportunity where others can't, see it where others don't, act while others hesitate, and demur when others plunge.'[3] They show weaknesses as well as strengths. They can identify items of crucial importance. They can help to expose the truth of the situation. They can stimulate vision.

Often a single number catches a person's imagination. Paul Yonggi Cho, the pastor of the world's largest church in Seoul, South Korea, now with a membership of 625,000 people, started with a church of 3,000 people. St Paul's Cathedral when it needed repairs in the 1970s appealed for one million pounds and measured all its response against that figure. Hudson Taylor was moved to the depths as he considered the one million Chinese who died each year without Christ. Bracknell Baptist Church built a church to seat 1,000 people — the one figure summarises the vision of what they wish to achieve.

If statistics are valuable, what are they saying? In this next section I analyse some key trends relevant to any church or Christian organisation.

1: THE CHURCH IS GROWING WORLD-WIDE

Christianity is alive and well around the world. An estimated six million Christians join the church in Africa every year. Five thousand new congregations are planted every twelve months in Latin America. One hundred years ago there were few Christians in Korea. Today, an estimated 25% of South Korea is Christian, and 47% of the Armed Forces. Forty years ago in Singapore there were relatively few Christians; today 60% of the doctors and 40% of the teachers are Christian. Even twenty years ago who would have expected 20,000 missionaries *from* Third World countries to be engaged in cross-cultural evangelism?[4]

The Revd Tom Houston, past President of World Vision International, suggests there are three key trends in the church world-wide in the last twenty-five years:

First there is the incredible growth of the Pentecostal church world-wide, documented so carefully by Peter Wagner.[5] He has shown how this church has multiplied in every continent in the world, until in 1985 there were an estimated 85 million denominational Pentecostals world-wide, excluding Chinese Pentecostals of perhaps 42 million and 66 million Protestant and Catholic charismatics. In 1975, Pentecostals and charismatics formed perhaps 8% of the world's Christian people; ten years later they had grown to be 19%. Of course he attributes this primarily to the blessing of the Lord, but also commends as important reasons for the growth their avid evangelism in taking the Gospel to people in the streets; to their policy of planting new congregations quickly; to their willingness to trust people with leadership without necessarily first passing through any specific course of training; the strong pastoral concern of their leaders; the liveliness of their worship with its heavy emphasis on participation, their widespread healing ministry, and what he calls the *'power encounter'*, or meeting with the Holy Spirit.[6]

Second there is the rapidly increasing number of Christian organisations – 'para-church agencies' as they are sometimes called, because they seek to work alongside the churches. This is certainly true in the United Kingdom. The 1983

edition of the *UK Christian Handbook* listed 2,400 organisations. Six years later the 1989/90 edition of the same *Handbook* listed nearly 4,100 organisations, and while some of the
difference is accounted for by organisations unintentionally
omitted in 1983, at least half of the difference is new organisations – equivalent to a new one being formed every other
working day.

Finally Tom Houston draws attention to the willingness of
Christian people to work together more co-operatively than
competitively: for instance, the larger relief organisations in
Britain jointly appeal for money; many para-church agencies
are interdenominational; people from different backgrounds
work happily together in organisations like the World Evangelical Fellowship, or the programmes of the Lausanne Committee on World Evangelisation.

But the world is not standing still. World-wide church
growth takes place against a background of increasing injustice. How can anyone remain placid when 83% of the
world's wealth is used by 25% of the world's population?[7]
When the Third World sees only 6% of the world's expenditure on health, and 15% of the expenditure on energy? Many
Christians, like Ron Sider in his book *Rich Christians in an
Age of Hunger*, have pointed out the sheer social injustice of
what's happening. Amos's ancient words still have modern
power, 'But let justice roll down like waters, and righteousness like an everflowing stream' (Amos 5:24, RSV).

Then too, there is increasing urbanisation. Five per cent of
the world lived in cities in 1880. By 1980 that had increased to
35%, but such is the pace of the movement that by the year
2000 it is estimated that perhaps 70% of the world's population will be attached to an urban conurbation. Who can
imagine a Mexico City of 32 million people? It is 19 million
now, and almost choked to death with cars and air pollution.
It is worth noting that this trend is not reflected in Britain; in
1965 41% of the population lived in a metropolitan area, in
1985 it was 36%.

The world's population passed the five billion mark in July
1987 according to the American Population Crisis Committee, and is due to hit the six billion mark in the late 1990s,

so that by the turn of the century the world-wide population will be approximately 6.2 billion. That means one billion more people in the world than at present. The weight of increase is accruing in South East Asia, so that by the year 2000 58% of the world's people will be Asian.

Increasing Christianity? David Barrett's mammoth work, the *World Christian Encyclopaedia*,[8] shows that about a third of the world's population has some kind of allegiance to the Christian faith. His work is mainly based on 1970 figures extrapolated to the year 2000, and shows a slightly decreasing proportion from 34.4% in 1900 to 32.3% in 2000. His figures exclude the phenomenal growth of the church in China however, which has only been evident in the last ten years. Including these figures (depending on what number is taken for China's Christians – many say perhaps fifty million) would change the downward trend to a slight increase. Today there are many movements determined to evangelise the world by the year 2000. A consultation bringing many of these advocates together was held in Singapore in January 1989. Tom Forrest, the energetic priest based in the Vatican, has a vision that will mean 'a birthday present for Jesus in 2000 AD of at least half the world Christian'. If fulfilled, Christianity will certainly be increasing rapidly in the next decade.

2: CHANGING BRITISH CULTURES

The world is changing; so is the United Kingdom, but not necessarily in the same way. In an article in the *Methodist Recorder*,[9] Revd Dr Donald English helpfully indicated some of the changes taking place, and the church's response to them. He pointed first to the potential of high visibility evangelism, like Mission England and Mission to London, and that significant numbers responded openly. Second he mentioned the growing numbers of Christian leaders speaking out on social and political issues, like the Ethiopian drought, or the miners' strike, and suggested that it was better to speak out than remain silent. Third he cited the ambitious radio and television programmes looking at Christianity pro-

vocatively. There is a need to stand for the truth and engage in
apologetics. Finally he drew attention to the influence of
television on our culture, as also indicated in Colin Morris's
book *God-in-a-Box*. It is important to determine criteria for
truth when it is depicted by fleeting images.

But behind these church changes other ones, which include
the following, are taking place:

Changing technology. We are in the middle of an increasing
alteration in the basic technology of our western civilisation.
Bill Gates, Chairman of the Microsoft Corporation, states
that technology is leading us into unprecedented territory at
an unprecedented pace. We cannot extrapolate from the past
to establish the rate of change in the future. 'The leap will be
unique.'[10] The space age has not just brought the stars into
view, but has brought a range of aids undreamt of by previous
generations. By the twenty-first century your church could be
operating a dozen computers. Who would have thought even
twenty years ago of portable computers? Or cameras which
can be concealed in the gem stone on a ring? Or even to have a
'chip' in your washing machine? If you buy an expensive car,
you buy perhaps five computers to help it run more effi-
ciently. Many factories use robots to help with production.
Most, if not all, of these mechanistic aids are neutral in their
essence. But it is all too easy to turn them to undesirable
practices. For example, a recent survey suggested that perhaps 39% of twelve to fifteen-year olds whose parents have a
video recorder use it to watch horror movies.[11]

Changing education. The education system is changing: for
instance the new GCSE examination for sixteen-year olds
introduced in the late 1980s and the 1988 Education Act. Will
this change the one child in six who needs special education?
School governors are now more responsible and the head
teachers have also been given much greater financial accountability. The emphasis is now on success, and results of exam-
inations have to be published regularly. The education
process gives the foundation for life; how then do we ensure
its compatibility with Christian standards? It remains to be

seen whether the compulsion of starting each day with a time of worship will help. The advent of television has partly challenged the broad methodology of education – not just more visual but also an approach which looks at many facets of a subject quickly before one explores in depth. What does this mean for Christian educationalists? We also need to rethink our ways of communicating. Christian videos are frequently more popular with young people than Christian books for example – which has direct implications for the Christian publishing industry. For example, one large church on the south coast found that their teenagers read only two Christian books a year.[12] In another large church a survey showed that only 44% of the children of Christian parents used their take-home Sunday School materials during the week, though how far this related to the particular type of materials used was not clear.[13]

Changing religion. Radio One used to have a 'Pause for Thought' item every day in which a Bible reading, hymn and prayer were used. It still does have a religious slot but now they offer your horoscope twice each day. The composition of the religious population in Britain has also changed. Nearly 3% of the population is Muslim, and 5% more belong to other non-Christian religions or non-Trinitarian churches like Jehovah's Witnesses, Mormons, Christadelphians and so on.[14] This 8% of the population relates to 1987, and has grown from 3% in 1970; it is likely to be 10% by the year 2000. With this goes an increasing interest in the occult. Ouija boards and tarot cards are seen in many schools. The number of Satanists is estimated at 16,000 and the number is growing. Our religious environment is changing, and we need to rethink what we mean by the uniqueness of our faith and how we communicate it.

Changing morality. In 1966 there were 35,000 divorces in Britain. By 1986 that number had become 180,000, and in 25% of these one or both partners had already experienced a divorce.[15] It is estimated that one young woman in ten will have had an abortion by the time she is twenty. Some 4,000 abortions took place on women under the age of twenty in 1987. Fifty per cent of women have lost their virginity by the age of sixteen, and it is thought only 8% of women are virgins on their wedding day.[16] Figures for men are not known, but are probably not very different. The breakdown of traditional values over the sanctity of marriage is extensive and has happened fast – one child in four is now illegitimate, almost a tripling of the percentage in ten years.

Changing society. Violence is increasing, and the public is much more conscious of it. In 1893, 9% of all offences were for burglary and robbery; by 1986 this proportion had increased to 25%, and with that the amount of violence involved.[17] The number of crimes has also increased dramatically this century, with some 3.8 million offences committed in 1986. The British Crime Survey suggests however that perhaps only a quarter of all crimes are reported.[18] Violence is seen not only among the football crowds, and in sporadic outbursts in rural areas, but also in the home. Some 50,000 children are mentally or physically abused each year. Fifty-two children were battered to death in 1982. The use of drugs has tripled in the last nine years, and one child in four is smoking regularly by the time they reach the age of fifteen.[19] We, who once were known for standing by our values, are now becoming known as the abortion centre of the world, an exporter of hooliganism and a profitable market for drug rings.[20] We also have a wealth polarisation, a North–South divide, and increasing racism.

Changing technology, education, religion, morality and society – all add up to a changing culture and we must come to *TERMS* with it. That means reconceptualising our message and making it more applicable to today's youth especially.

3: MEMBERSHIP DECLINE: ATTENDANCE INCREASE

Membership figures

The *UK Christian Handbook 1989/90 Edition* gives the following numbers of church members in the United Kingdom:

Table 1: Total UK Church members

	1970	1980	1990E	2000E
Anglican[1]	2,548,000	2,154,000	1,824,000	1,551,000
Methodist	694,000	558,000	509,000	482,000
Baptist	295,000	240,000	244,000	255,000
Presbyterian	1,807,000	1,509,000	1,288,000	1,135,000
Other Protestant	532,000	534,000	652,000	783,000
Roman Catholic[2]	2,715,000	2,343,000	1,949,000	1,657,000
Orthodox	193,000	209,000	232,000	252,000
TOTAL	8,784,000	7,546,000	6,699,000	6,114,000
Percentage of adult population	21%	17%	14%	13%

[1]Electoral Roll figures (adjusted)   E = Estimated
[2]Mass attendances

It is obvious that membership has decreased and will go on decreasing. Both Anglicans and Roman Catholics will see a drop of one million members between 1970 and 2000 if present trends continue, and this accounts for the majority of the decrease from 8.8 million members in 1970 to 6.1 million in 2000. Most of the rest is seen in the Presbyterian Church which is set to lose 670,000 members in the same period. It is important to note that the Methodist rate of decline is lessening: they dropped 130,000 in the 1970s, but only 47,000 in the 1980s, and if the trends prove accurate, will only drop 27,000 in the 1990s. The Baptists, while seeing a drop in membership of 45,000 in the 1970s, are set to grow perhaps 5,000 in the 1980s having reached as it were the bottom of the trough and are now coming out of it. If that continues they should

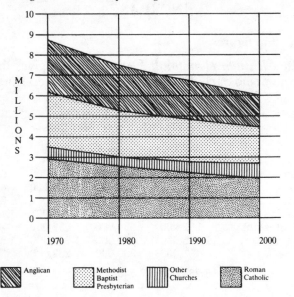

Fig 1: Membership change in British churches

increase a further 10,000 at least in the 1990s bringing them back to where they were in 1977 by the year 2000.

The growth areas are in the other Protestant churches – African/West Indian churches, the Independent churches which includes the House Church movement (or New Church or Kingdom Movement), the Pentecostal churches. Why has this growth taken place? Partly because these churches all emphasise participation in worship and sharing experience. Partly it is because many of these churches have a common identity factor – common colour, customs, culture or nationality. Churches are growing partly perhaps because of the size factor (to which I shall return), and partly because of their theology. Partly it is because of the emphasis on signs and wonders by some churches.[21] Churches of all types are growing: evangelical, Anglo-Catholic, Roman Catholic (especially in Wales), and the Orthodox. More growth is expected.

Attendance growth

Membership is one thing, but attendance is quite another, as the surveys published in the *Prospects* series show. These studies have concentrated in obtaining data directly from individual churches on church attendance; at the time of writing a further study of English churches is under way but the results from that are not yet available. To extrapolate attendance from a single survey across the same range of years as given in the *UK Christian Handbook* would be untenable, but the estimates in Table 2 seem reasonable, although they exclude Northern Ireland.

Table 2: Adult Church life in England, Wales and Scotland

	Attendance in thousands			Percentage change 1980–90	Membership in thousands			Percentage change 1980–90
	1980	1985	1990E	%	1980	1985	1990E	%
Anglican	1,337	1,306	1,281	−4	1,990	1,828	1,680	−16
Methodist	470	455	474	+1	498	465	448	−10
Baptist	260	271	284	+9	232	231	233	+0.5
Presbyterian	466	442	421	−10	1,227	1,108	1,030	−16
Other Churches	616	701	809	+31	514	547	620	+21
Total Protestant	3,149	3,175	3,269	+4	4,461	4,179	4,011	−10
Roman Catholic	1,969	1,775	1,620	−18	No equivalent figures			—
Orthodox	7	7	7	0	209	220	232	+11
Total Christian	5,125	4,957	4,896	−4	E = Estimate			

Table 2 shows that church attendance for Protestant churches has *increased* in the 1990s whereas church membership has *decreased*. Methodist attendance has increased, as also indicated in a 1988 report by David Bridge,[22] against a decline in membership. If the Methodist attendance continues to increase, their 1990 figures will show more attending than belonging. Baptist attendance has increased, and at a far faster rate than their membership. They have consistently had more people attending their church than members (120 attenders for every 100 members). It is however in the Other Churches (in fact the Independent churches) where attendance especially outstrips membership, although both have grown strongly during the 1980s. They have 130 attenders for every 100 members. This attendance growth is in the same denominations as the membership growth – the ethnic African/West Indian churches, House Churches, and Pentecostal churches.

It would be all too easy to get depressed by looking only at the membership figures: the attendance figures show a much more encouraging picture.

4: ELDERLY CHURCH-GOERS

Why is the church membership decreasing? The answer is that church members are dying off. The church has a relatively large number of elderly people. The age of church members is not known, but the *Prospects* surveys already mentioned asked for the age of church-goers. These show that 25% of *adults* attending church are sixty-five years of age or over against the population proportion of only 19%. We thus have a third as many elderly people in our churches than we might expect. Over the next twenty years or so these proportions will come closer together, with the church-going elderly reducing as a percentage of all church-goers, and the proportion of elderly adults in the population slightly increasing (to 20% by the year 2000).

Unfortunately elderly people die. A woman of sixty-five can expect to live another seventeen years, and a man of sixty-five, thirteen years. If they reach seventy-five they can expect to live only ten and eight years respectively.[23] There are 800,000 Protestant church-goers over the age of sixty-five. Suppose for purpose of illustration, that the average age of these in 1980 was seventy-two. Then the probability is that of these 800,000, 250,000 will have died by 1990. This would reduce the *entire* church-going population, for this reason alone, by 8%. The deaths of those under 65 would reduce churchgoers by a further 4%. So the fact that Protestant church-going has actually *increased* between 1980 and 1990 by 4% (Table 2) means that its true rate of increase is 16% (8+4+4) but 12% of this increase was offset by deaths. To this simple equation we must add the net effects of migration, plus the effects of conversion and the loss of those leaving the faith, or becoming too ill or moving too far away to attend regularly anymore. These last numbers are currently unquantifiable and are assumed (for simplicity) to balance out to zero change, though health factors alone would suggest a negative outflow if the figures were known. This rapid drop-out because of church people dying is likely to continue for at least another decade (7% of church-goers in 1990 are likely to die in the 1990s).

Table 3 gives the detailed figures, bearing in mind that they are all very tentative:

Table 3: Attendance by age and sex 1980 and 1990

Age of church-goers	1980 Attendance (Thousands)			Assumed average age	Percentage likely to die 1980–89		Residual 1990 Attendance of 1980 attenders (Thousands)			Percentage change 1980–90
	Men	*Women*	*Total*		*% Men*	*% Women*	*Men*	*Women*	*Total*	*%*
15–19	157	199	356	17	*0.9*	*0.3*	156	198	354	*−1*
20–29	196	252	448	25	*0.9*	*0.5*	194	251	445	*−1*
30–44	281	388	669	37	*2.2*	*1.5*	275	382	657	*−2*
45–64	380	496	876	55	*15*	*8.7*	323	453	776	*−11*
65 and over	300	500	800	72	*33*	*30*	200	350	550	*−31*
TOTAL	1,314	1,835	3,149				1,148	1,634	2,782	*−12*

If the same age-group proportions apply to church members as to church-goers – and it is unlikely there is a strict correspondence as church members are probably rather older than church-goers – then it would mean that 12% of church members would have died in the 1980s. Since the percentage decline was only 10% this means we have actually *gained* church members, but this is hidden by deaths. The small gain is however well within the margins of error in the many assumptions contained in Table 3.

Some of the older para-church agencies are currently enjoying a boom in their legacy income. The above figures give a possible explanation of that – a relatively large number of deaths of elderly people, which could continue for perhaps another decade.

How then do you increase church attendance? One way would be by helping elderly church-goers to live longer! But we should be encouraged by this analysis. Our vision for an enlarging church is happening and has just to be tempered by the fact that the Lord is actually in the business of peopling heaven not earth!

5: DECLINE OF NOMINAL CHRISTIANITY

A study undertaken in 1967 showed that 59% of people were converted in their teenage years.[24] If a person is seventy now, he or she was born immediately after the First World War and came to their impressionable teenage years, spiritually speaking, in the 1930s or 1940s. What was the world like then? Another war was in the air, with a massive build up of continuous tension as Hitler annexed one country after another in Europe. A fascinating doctoral thesis of H. M. Currie, published in *Churches and Church-goers*, now out of print, showed that people often went to church more when war occurred or during other national crises. Are we seeing today one aspect of the spiritual consequences of the Second World War?

During the 1930s a number of evangelists took campaigns in this country, like Billy Sunday. It was also a time when many were expected to go to church and did so. Sunday schools still attracted significant proportions of children each week and laid some kind of foundation. Were the 1930s and 1940s particularly different from the 1920s in this regard? Probably not, but they were significantly different from the 1960s and 1970s.

The 1930s were a time when nominal Christianity was very acceptable. People would be 'church people' but not necessarily believe. They would go to church but not necessarily believe all that the church taught. Many of these older people do not have clear scriptural theology even if they have had a great deal of church-going experience.

What do nominal Christians believe? Many surveys have

sought answers to such questions, and the norm of many such may be listed:[25]

1) *God*. Seventy-two per cent believe in God, who is seen as Love (91% of the 72), Creator (88%), Protector (79%), Father (75%), Redeemer (73%), and Sustainer (59%). God is thus seen as personal, not impersonal. In studies of those using the Central London YMCA Hotel, 58% of those aged 16–25 believed in God and 54% of those 26–39.[26]

2) *Jesus*. Eighty-nine per cent believe that Jesus Christ was 'someone special'; 43% that he was the Son of God, specially chosen by God (51% of the 43) or God in human form (40% of the 43). Forty-four per cent of YMCA users aged 16–25 believed Jesus was the Son of God, falling to 40% for those aged 26–39.

3) *Life after Death*. Seventy-six per cent had thought about whether there is life after death, but of these only 40% believed in it. Forty-four per cent did not believe, and 16% did not know. Forty-three per cent of the YMCA sample aged 16–25 also believed in life after death and 38% aged 26–39. Of these 76% said it helped them to make sense of life. Sixty-four per cent thought everyone had some kind of life after death, but not the same for everyone.

Why today are there so many nominal Christians? Or, rephrasing the question, why is there so much secularism in our Christianity? David Lyon, the sociologist, has attempted to answer this question, and gave the following reasons:[27]

1) A *'loss of faith'*, although he says, 'it might not be quite such a plausible term once we know *why* our Victorian forebears went to church.'

2) A *loss of uniqueness*. 'The Christian religion no longer enjoys the unique and privileged position it once held in Western society', but it is the social context of the growth of relativism, and the increasing number of religious options which are critically important.

3) A *loss of intellectual confidence*. If Darwin really disproves God it is because people are willing to accept that argument, which is related not just to the intellect

but the whole social and cultural framework within which the argument is made.

4) *A loss of religion.* Those who, like Max Webber, feel the Western world is inexorably driving itself along the road of rationalisation, intellectualisation and disenchantment, may simply be selecting those conditions antipathetic to religion which result from their own religious preference. In other words, because they have lost religion they see the world as losing religion.

5) *Marginalisation*, which affects the character of religion in that it focuses the growth of double standards and role-split lives.

6) *Privatisation*, in that religion becomes essentially associated with the world of home and family, an appropriate leisure time pursuit. As Melanie Cottrell puts it,[28] 'Identity for middle-class people is divorced from social structure, and . . . people are forced in upon themselves'.

7) *A pendulum church* which swings backwards and forwards because it is in tension – between those who cling to the bureaucratic denominations and those who prefer 'destructured spontaneity'.

Os Guinness would support these implications of secularisation, though phrasing it differently. The essential damage to the church, he would say, is that relating not to the crisis of credibility but 'a crisis of its plausibility (whether Christianity *seems* true, not whether it *is* true)'. There is a large gap between the church's 'spiritual rhetoric and its social reality'.[29]

'Luckmann is substantially right[30] about the fate of church religion in modern society. It is privatised and its claims have no real bearing on everyday life. Even for committed religious people, the world is organised in such a way that unless a career is chosen which has close links with the ethos of Christianity (the caring professions), religion does not, and perhaps cannot determine the priorities of everyday life.'[31]

In North America, George Gallup Jnr has undertaken a series of surveys, and from these he identifies four trends which threaten to undermine the effectiveness of the church:

1) A serious lack of knowledge about the central tenets of religion and religious heritage.
2) An easy credulity or gullibility that allows regular church-goers to hold contrary beliefs (for example, church-goers believe in astrology as much as non-church-goers).
3) A lack of spiritual discipline as seen, for example, in a prayer life without structure, focus or intensity.
4) An anti-intellectual tendency which promotes empty emotionalism rather than the blending of mind and heart.[32]

Thus we see a decline of religion. But, as C. S. Lewis observed in writing on this subject:[33] 'The "decline of religion" becomes a very ambiguous phenomenon. One way of putting the truth would be that the religion which has declined was not Christianity. It was a vague Theism with a strong and virile ethical code which, far from standing over against the "World", was absorbed into the whole fabric of English institutions and sentiment and therefore demanded church-going as (at best) a part of loyalty and good manners or (at worst) a proof of respectability . . . The new freedom first allowed accurate observations to be made. When no man goes to church except because he seeks Christ the number of actual believers can at last be discovered . . .

'The decline of "religion", thus understood, seems to me in some ways a blessing. At the very worst it makes the issue clear . . . The fog of "religion" has lifted; the positions and numbers of both armies can be observed; and real shooting is now possible.'

6: AN INCREASING LOSS OF BEHAVIOURAL COMMITMENT

Just over a quarter (actually 26%) of the UK population are strictly outside the Christian and other religious communities – over 14 million people in Great Britain. That is a large number. Not all will necessarily have always been outside, however.

In a brilliant study called simply *The Unchurched*,[34] Professor Hale analyses ten groups of people to whom he spoke in a six-month residential study who were then beyond the Church. All *were* outside the Church when he talked with them, but as his classifications are described below, note how many were once inside. Most consider themselves 'believers', if not 'belongers'. Few are without 'religious memories'.

The anti-institutionalists. Those who are defectors from the church on the basis of what they perceive to be the church's preoccupation with its own self-maintenance. They may object to the political nature of the church, its form of government, or its leadership. They may find the liturgies too emotional or too objective and cold. They frequently object to the church's emphasis on finance, building and property. They think of themselves as solitary Christians or unaffiliated fellow-travellers. They perceive that the churches have lost the 'spiritual point of religion'.

The boxed-in. Those who found past experiences in a church as too confining. They were mostly church members once, but have now left. Narrow doctrine or prescriptive ethics may have smothered them. They might feel stifled, resentful that the church continues to treat them as a child, or adolescent. They view the church as a box that limits their freedom to 'do my own thing' or to 'do it my way'. Often the university student or the newly liberated woman is counted in this company.

The burned-out. Those whose energies have been utterly consumed by the church. They have known the inside and it has depleted their resources, talents and time. They may feel they have been exploited or manipulated. They were unintentionally overly involved without space or time for respite. Or they sought leadership and accepted too much. They are now 'worked out' and weary of the continual demands they feel will be made if they maintain affiliation.

THE CONTEXT OF VISION

The floaters. These were never really committed to the church in the first place. They never put an anchor down in the church community. Their involvement was peripheral. They may lack any deep feelings for or sensitivity toward what the churches stand for, say, or do. The church fails to make any impression on their minds or hearts. They are indifferent to the point of saying 'I couldn't care less'. Or they may fear the demands of responsibility to others or to programmes. They never opt in sufficiently to own for themselves what the church teaches. When inside, they are really on the outside. Essentially, they cop out, in the sense of withholding commitment, involvement or meaningful ties.

The hedonists. These are those who seek fulfilment of life's purpose in momentary pleasures or a succession of pleasure-satisfying activities. Thus church membership becomes an intrusion on their time, as one who is a participant or spectator of those things that 'turn one on'. The church 'doesn't want me to have a good time', or 'compared to other excitements, the church can't compete'.

The locked-out. Those who feel the churches have closed their doors against them either via formal excommunication, slight, disregard, or discrimination, overt or covert. They believe the churches for various reasons do not want them inside. Although some may have locked themselves out, the effect is the same. They may express deep hurt that their desire for full communication or fellowship has been limited, possibly because of divorce or disapproved family planning practices, or persistent shunning of a church's moral codes. They may feel slighted, overlooked, disregarded, forgotten and lost. They may feel they have been deliberately excluded. They believe persons 'of their kind' are not wanted, often frozen out, snubbed or openly excluded. They often include the poor, the elderly, those with unconventional life-styles, minorities and others 'on the fringe'.

The nomads. These are the people who never stay in one place long enough to call it home, perhaps because of occupational mobility. As a consequence they feel themselves to be in virtual exile, a diaspora from the homeland. They can find no church in their present community with any semblance of or continuity with their past church affiliations. Their unchurchedness is a function of their minority religious preferences.

The pilgrims. These describe their religious beliefs as in the process of formation. They are on an ideological pilgrimage, searching for satisfying meanings and values. They fear premature closure. They expect to be tolerated by others for their own inchoate or imperfectly formed beliefs. They refuse to be described as secularists, humanists or agnostics. They are locked into no position but are open to all. Their central characteristic is tentativeness.

The publicans. These are the largest group of unchurched. They perceive the churches to be primarily populated by pharisees. They call those within the churches hypocrites, phoneys, and persons living double lives. This dissonance becomes, for them, a scandal. They perceive a discrepancy between what church members profess to believe and their performance in society. Of themselves, they say in effect: 'If we cannot live up to expectations, we prefer to stay on the outside. There are already too many half-hearted on the inside.'

The true unbelievers. These include the atheists and agnostics who deny the existence of any ultimate reality or hold that any such reality is unknown or unknowable. They include also the rationalists and deists whose theology, formally or informally articulated, is based on human reason rather than revelation. They include also the humanists and secularists who embrace worldliness, in the sense that the dignity or worth of people lies in their capacity for self-realisation through reason, without benefit of supernatural revelation, of clergy or of church.

Since many in these categories will overlap with nominal church membership, it is worth asking, is there any evidence of behavioural changes once a person opts out of regular church attendance or membership? This question has not been researched in any depth, but in an interesting chapter Roozen and Carroll[35] suggest that one critical difference between ongoing church attendance and those who are now outside is a definite commitment to Jesus Christ. This could form the *crucial key*, but the same study shows two in five of those now unchurched would say they too had once made a commitment to Christ. We must therefore beware of what Alan Flavelle calls 'defective commitment'. He exemplifies this by quoting Sir John Lawrence, a leading Anglican, who said, 'What does the average church member want? He wants a building that looks like a church . . . services of the kind he's been used to . . and ministers who dress in the way he approves of . . . and to be left alone!'[36]

When Melanie Cottrell interviewed middle-class people at length she found a few for whom religion was 'a central life-value'. She wrote, 'They all have a definite transcendent goal or aim. Their lives display what might be described as dedication to a cause.' In contrast, the non-religious church-goers had 'no dedication to a life-project'. Their religion was highly theistic with few behavioural consequences.

Some would say that the oneness of the Body of Christ is not dependent on formal membership. A non-member can be, and is accepted as, a part of the Body provided he or she is *actively involved*. But this is not traditional teaching. Ed Dayton [37] notes that 'statistics show that although the number of those who claim to be born again continues to rise, ten to twenty million of them are not members of a local church. The biblical concept that Christians are all part of one body apparently is outside their understanding. The institutional church is losing its legitimacy.' As noted above, it is becoming secularised, and that secularisation is seen in a loss of commitment.

This is reinforced by Edward Bailey in his (as yet unpublished) thesis on Winterbourne Parish in which he describes the differences between the Regulars, the Occasional and the Lapsed. The Occasional miss a full church and the enjoyment of worship that goes with that; that their irregularity is part of the cause of the effect they deprecate is unnoticed. The Lapsed used to come, and may well feel guilty about not coming, but friends or relations, or other events, have come between them and even occasional attendance. Dr Bailey indicates that their explanation 'contains more remorse than resolution. Its dominant note is self-doubt.'[38] What has happened? In a nutshell, they have *lost their commitment*, or their willingness to translate their belief into action.

7: THE FRAGMENTING OF RELIGIOUS AFFILIATION

We have strayed some way from the issue of trends in order to look at the phenomenon of nominalism more closely. The religious structure of the British population may be charted as follows:

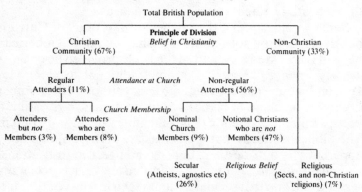

Fig 2: Religious structure of population

Total British Population

Principle of Division
Belief in Christianity

Christian Community (67%) — Non-Christian Community (33%)

Attendance at Church

Regular Attenders (11%) — Non-regular Attenders (56%)

Church Membership

Attenders but *not* Members (3%) — Attenders who are Members (8%) — Nominal Church Members (9%) — Notional Christians who are *not* Members (47%)

Religious Belief

Secular (Atheists, agnostics etc) (26%) — Religious (Sects, and non-Christian religions) (7%)

Percentages relate to the year 1980

This table is illustrated on the left-hand side of Figure 3 opposite. Those in the Christian 'community' are 67% of the population. The outer square represents the population, the inner circle the proportion in the Christian community.

However a change is taking place. Those who go to church but who do not belong, tend to join. Those who go to church and are members, tend to stop going. Those who are members of a church but who do not go, tend to stop being members. Those who consider themselves Christian but who do not belong or go to church tend to stop thinking of themselves as Christian. These four broad movements are not of equal weight and will not always occur to any one individual in a lifetime. Perhaps a particular person will only go through two of these four stages. But the net effect would be one of loss were it not for the fact that new Christians are constantly being recruited.

If these trends continue in their existing proportions, however, the change over a generation will be dramatic and by the year 2015 the church may well be as shown on the right-hand side of Figure 3.

Fig 3: The changing religious community in the UK

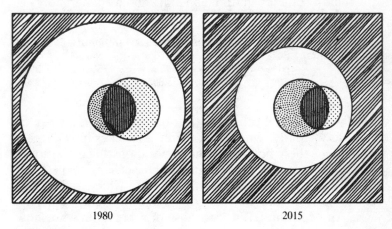

1980   2015

Goers, not yet members.

Goers, who are also members.

Members who are not regular church-goers.

By 2015 there will be an increasing identification of Christianity with one particular behavioural manifestation of it –

that of church-going. The diagram also suggests that the number of people who belong to a church but who do not go will become relatively small, and the proportion of people who go to church but who do not belong will become larger. The numbers who are outside regular attendance and membership and yet still feel themselves part of the Christian population is greatly diminished. What in fact has happened is that the United Kingdom has moved from a nominally Christian to a definitely non-Christian society. The large bulk of the population are totally outside the faith.

Essentially the reason is that the nominal Christians of today beget the non-Christians of tomorrow. One of the most intriguing questions asked in the Leeds Project related to the religion of the interviewee's parents and grandparents. There was little variation between the sexes, but the generation gap was as follows, disallowing those who replied 'Don't know':

Table 4: Change in Christian affiliation by generation

	Anglicans	Other Protestants	Roman Catholics	Non-Christian religions	No religion
Grandparents	60%	14%	20%	5%	1%
Parents	61%	14%	17%	5%	3%
Self	28%	13%	28%	8%	23%

Clearly the Anglicans have lost out in the present generation very greatly, whereas the Free Churches have largely maintained their hold over the generations. The Catholics show an interesting set of figures and perhaps suggest the special influence of grandparents. The non-Christian increase relates more to the 'newer' groups like the Jehovah's Witnesses or Mormons. But it is those of no religion who show the greatest increase, and take up much of the drop in the Anglican figures. This tallies with the declining Anglican community. The Anglican church has the greatest number of liberal ministers, and Steve Bruce[39] and David Martin[40] have shown elsewhere the consequential fall away resulting from such a theology.

One of the questions included in the annual British Social

Attitudes Study[41] asked if a person was Christian, and if so, their denomination. They also asked if their position had changed since they were a child under sixteen. Results from the 1984 study were:

Table 5: Change in Christian affiliation in a lifetime

	Anglicans	Other Protestants	Roman Catholics	Non-Christian religions	No religion
As a child	43%	20%	11%	2%	24%
Now	40%	16%	10%	2%	32%

This table confirms the decline in Anglicanism found in Leeds, but also suggests a decline in other Protestant denominations and the Roman Catholics; with a similar, but smaller increase in those with no religion. But an increase from 24% to 32% still represents a considerable drift away.

When did such a drift away occur? Sixty per cent of the Leeds interviewees said it was when they 'grew up'. The relatively high child attendance figures confirm the desire of many children to learn about God and church. Yet 88% of the Leeds sample indicated that the way they were brought up was one of the reasons for making them the kind of person they were. Religious traditions, especially empty formalism, presumably apart!

David Barrett's massive *World Christian Encyclopaedia* looks at the progress of Christianity in a number of different ways. As well as Christian adherents he also talks of 'practising church people', that is, those who have a rather higher degree of commitment. In the last twenty years of the twentieth century many countries in Western Europe are forecast to have a decline in this category, and not only those in Britain.

He also looks at the number of individual church congregations. In many parts of Europe these will be static, though in a few countries they are slightly increasing. In Iceland, the Benelux countries, Austria, and Spain, the number of congregations is set to increase at least 5% between 1980 and 2000. The emerging picture is therefore of rather more churches, but smaller churches as there are fewer people.

David Barrett also looks at the number of denominations, or separate church groups that will form in the last twenty years of the century. Half of the countries in Western Europe are estimated to have an increase of at least 20% in their number of denominations between 1980 and 2000. The picture, therefore, that emerges is not just of smaller and more numerous churches, but also of more insular ones. It is perhaps this change which will have the greatest impact if it comes true. More attention will be given by individual churches to their doctrinal position, to their own administration, and their support will be primarily for their own networks rather than perhaps for more working together with faiths across the world. Thus we will have an increasingly fragmented European Church.

8: SMALLER CHURCHES, FEWER MINISTERS

Church size seems to have something to do with church growth, though the relationship is at best tenuous.[42] Church sizes usefully fall into three types: small (under 50 in the normal Sunday congregation), medium (between 50 and 150), large (over 150). The proportion of churches in each category, as given by the *Prospects* surveys are:

Table 6: Size of churches

All except Catholic	Small	Medium	Large
England	61%	31%	8%
Wales	77%	21%	2%
Scotland	37%	36%	27%
Overall	61%	30%	9%
Catholic churches			
England	5%	13%	82%
Wales	12%	27%	61%
Scotland	10%	17%	73%
Overall	6%	14%	80%

Small churches can be cohesive, warm and attractive. You are missed if you don't go and every person is expected to play his or her part. Many small ethnic or House Church congregations started with few people and began to grow. However, the typical small church is rural with fewer than fifty members, a shared minister, and a service less frequent than weekly. Such churches can become quickly exhausted by having to maintain a large and ageing building, and their vision tends to be much more one of maintenance than expansion. It is all too easy in such circumstances to have too ambitious a programme.

Medium-sized churches are frequently those with a single person as a full-time minister. Almost one third of all the churches in Great Britain are this size. Often a one-man pastorate can become a self-limiting factor as the church attendance moves towards the upper limit. There are only so many people any person can remember.[43] In such situations if the church is to grow it needs additional professional help – not necessarily always an assistant minister, but perhaps a church administrator, church secretary, youth officer or pastoral worker. The numbers of such churches, which were growing in England in the late 1970s, show their potential. They have sufficient numbers to give back-up resources, and are able if they wish to engage in an attractive evangelistic ministry with enough people to make it a team effort.

Large churches often are growing churches. They need a different style of leadership. The minister must be able to work with a team, delegating to others. Invariably there will be other full-time personnel, so the leadership structure must watch the work to be done. Organisational resources are usually available in such a church, so the programme becomes the more important, and with that, the vision of the leader.

Ministerial shortage

Church membership is increasing but so many are 'going to glory' as the Salvation Army reminds us that the actual

numbers are declining. But church attendance is positively
increasing. So what of leadership? In 1985 the number of
ministers in Britain was given in the *UK Christian Handbook*
as 39,500; a number which is decreasing slightly as shown in
Table 7 below.

Table 7: Number of ministers

	Number in 1970	Net change between 1970 and 1985	Number in 1985	Estimated net change between 1985 and 2000	Estimated number in 2000
Anglican	17,400	−3,300	14,100	−1,500	12,600
Methodist	4,500	−700	3,800	−500	3,300
Baptist	2,500	−100	2,400	+200	2,600
Presbyterians	4,200	−700	3,500	−400	3,100
Other Churches	6,400	+2,900	9,300	+2,800	12,100
Total Protestant	35,000	−1,900	33,100	+600	33,700
Roman Catholic	8,100	−1,900	6,200	−1,000	5,200
Orthodox	100	+100	200	+100	300
Total churches	43,200	−3,700	39,500	−300	39,200

The Anglicans lost many ministers in the 1970s. The loss
reflected retirements after the very large numbers of ordinands in the years following the Second World War. The
continuing drop in numbers in the 1980s and 1990s reflects
retirements after the larger increases in ordinands in the early
1960s which were almost certainly as a result of the Billy
Graham Crusades in the mid-1950s. The numbers assume,
however, that at least 200 clergy transfer back per year into
the pastoral home ministry after serving overseas as missionaries, as chaplains or elsewhere. The forecast numbers also
assume an average per year of 325 ordinands, who complete
training adequately. A more recent publication by the Ministry Co-ordinating Group forecasts a larger drop.[44] The number of evangelicals emerging from the Anglican training
colleges is increasing and stood at 51% of those in full-time
training in 1988.[45]

The Methodists saw fewer retirements of ministers proportionately than the Anglicans between 1970 and 1985 as they

had more younger men, but this will begin to change as the century closes, as Table 8 shows.[46]

Table 8: Age of ministers

	Anglicans 1971	Anglicans 1984	Methodists 1986
Under 30	8%	5%	3%
30–39	20%	22%	17%
40–49	20%	28%	31%
50–59	26%	29%	36%
60 or over	26%	16%	13%
Average age in years	49.0	48.3	48.9

The Baptists, having seen a drop in ministerial numbers in the 1970s, are set to gain them back in the 1990s. The Orthodox are experiencing a steady growth in numbers.

It is the Other Churches category that is again seeing growth – this time in personnel. Not all of this is in the House Church movement however. Of the 2,900 increase between 1970 and 1985 in Table 7, fewer than 700 are House Church leaders. 1,600 of the new ministers are African/West Indian, whose policy is to have many ministers per church (on average about five); as new congregations grow so do the number of their leaders, many in a part-time capacity. In this period there was also an increase of 450 Pentecostal ministers. The ethnic church leadership is expected to continue to grow between 1985 and 2000 – of the projected 2,800, 1,100 are African/West Indian. But the estimates include an expected increase of House Church Movement ministers by a further 1,400, and the Pentecostal under 200.

Both the Presbyterians and the Catholics are seeing a steady drop in the number of ministers and priests throughout the thirty years between 1970 and 2000, 26% for the Presbyterian ordained manpower, and 36% for Catholic priests (against 28% for the Anglicans). These drops have met severe criticism from some. The Revd Gerald Arbuckle, writing on 'Pastoral Research'[47] says, 'The Church is pastorally adrift, without a vision rooted in the needs of the people . . . The fact that no well-researched national or regional plans exist to cope with the dramatic downturn in vocations to the priesthood and religious life reinforces this conclusion'.

What are the implications behind these trends?

1) The increasing stress for ministers when replacement clergy or assistant curates are not available. It means fewer people will be tempted to do more work to keep everything going. Ministers may be pushed to the extreme that can cause burn-out. In the interim it often means narrowing vision to a maintenance activity rather than finding the energy for expansion or development.

2) It probably also means that additional training would be useful for existing clergy so that they are better equipped to handle the management of their time, determining priorities, learning to work better with teams, knowing how to motivate others, and how to build realistic visions.

3) The situation suggests structural problems for the main institutional churches which are experiencing the severest drops. The amalgamation of parishes is one answer to this problem and not always the most satisfactory. Experiments with Local Ecumenical Projects are under way in many areas, some successfully and others less so. The Presbyterians and Methodists already have women ministers, the Anglicans seem likely to have some during the 1990s, but women priests are not likely to be a solution followed by the Catholics. There is currently an upsurge in the number of 'Non-stipendiary Ministers' in the Anglican church – effectively part-time ministers who do a secular job during the week and act as a minister at the weekend. This may prove a partial solution.

4) Devolving power to lay people seems an inevitable consequence. How realistically such teams of 'volunteers' can be built and used, how much training and guidance will be needed will vary from church to

church. Some have already highly effective teams of high calibre people, who are well able to run most, if not all, the affairs of the local church, whereas others have some way to go. A few denominations, like the Christian Brethren, rely almost entirely on lay people. The emphasis is on delegation and on leadership. Lay people have to be given permission to succeed in their assignments – something that makes some ministers feel very threatened.

9: FINANCIAL CONCERNS

From church staffing we move to para-church agency income. The total monies given by church people to their churches, for whatever purpose, is not available. The larger churches do publish such information and some of the smaller denominations, especially in Scotland and Northern Ireland, also do. But the ethnic churches, House Churches, Pentecostal and other independent churches mostly do not, and hence the overall amounts given are not known. Nor is the purpose for which such money is given usually known – whether to support the local church ministry or the wider missionary work of the world-wide church. Hence I have confined myself in this section to looking at the recipients rather than the givers, the many para-church organisations who receive a substantial amount of money each year. This detail is based on successive editions of the *UK Christian Handbook*.

The crisis of vision is nowhere expressed more pragmatically than in the giving patterns of God's people. While the total giving has increased substantially, its distribution is also changing significantly.

Total income. How much has actually been given to Christian organisations? Table 9 gives details, with the last column indicating total income since 1981 which had increased only at the rate of the Retail Price Index (RPI), or cost-of-living index as it is popularly called. Total income given to Christian organisations has comfortably beaten the RPI and presents a

lot of money – although only 0.27% of the country's Gross
National Product (or total wealth).

Table 9: Total money given to Christian organisations

	As Measured £m	Grossed Up £m	Grossed Up Index	RPI	Total at RPI Rate £m
1981	307	350	100	100	350
1983	397	475	136	114	399
1985	584	600	171	127	445
1987	703	750	214	136	476

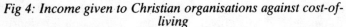

Fig 4: Income given to Christian organisations against cost-of-living

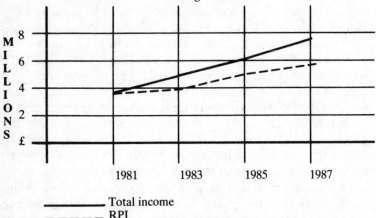

Income and number of organisations. The index given in
Table 9 shows that 1983 income was 36% up on 1981 and the
1985 income was 71% up on 1981 and that these increases
beat the the Retail Price Index by a wide margin; likewise the
1987 income. However this growth reflects an increasing
number of organisations, as is shown below:

Table 10: Total money given to Christian organisations compared with the number of organisations

	Number of Organis- ations	Organis- ations Index	Average Income per Organis- ation	Average Income Index	RPI	Average at RPI Rate
1981	2,402	100	£145,712	100	100	£145,712
1983	2,989	124	£158,916	109	114	£166,000
1985	3,580	149	£167,598	115	127	£185,000
1987	4,074	170	£184,094	126	136	£198,000

Fig 5: Income per organisation against cost-of-living

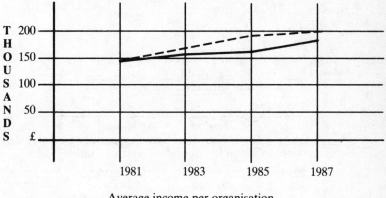

———————— Average income per organisation

– – – – – RPI

Table 10 shows that the average income per Christian organisation in the United Kingdom has not kept pace with inflation. In other words, although the actual total given to Christian organisations has increased considerably during the 1980s, so has the number of Christian organisations, and when one takes the increasing number of organisations into account, the average amount given to each organisation has not kept pace with the rate of inflation. In fact the increased amount of giving with respect to the number of organisations is only about two-thirds the increase which would be required to keep up with the rate of inflation. Thus it could be argued that the increasing number of new organisations – inevitably by their very nature small organisations – is actually doing Christian work as a whole a disservice, because it deflects support that might otherwise be given to established work. Clearly this argument cannot be pushed to its limits since there will always be the need for new organisations to keep pace with the changing environment. But we should ask whether the present multiplication of societies is the only option.

Giving by church members. Although the total amount of money given, of the order of £750,000,000 in 1987, is not an inconsequential sum, it is not a large amount per individual when averaged by the number of church members as Table 11 below shows:

Table 11: Total money given to Christian organisations by Church members

	Estimate total giving £m	Estimated Total Number of Church Members	Giving per member per year	Giving Index	Earnings Index
1981	350	7,423,000	£47	100	100
1983	475	7,251,328	£66	139	125
1985	600	7,055,150	£85	180	148
1987	750	6,926,723	£108	230	172

The implication of Table 11 is that people have been increasing the amount of their giving on average in the 1980s. In fact the average amount given per member has more than doubled from £47 in 1981 to £108 in 1987. When you compare this increased rate of giving with the rate of increase in average earnings, also given in Table 11, it is clear that the actual amounts being given are increasing proportionately

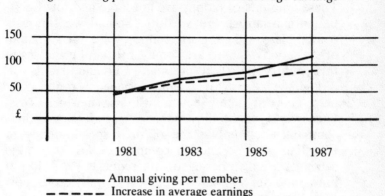

Fig 6: Giving per church member and average earnings

——————— Annual giving per member
— — — — — Increase in average earnings

more than their income. This raises the questions: is the increased giving because church members are giving more or is it because non-church members are giving more to Christian organisations?

Whatever the answers, some implications of these figures are:

1) The need for much more teaching on the responsibilities and duties of stewardship. While the figures given above exclude private giving to individual churches, it is still quite clear that the average level of giving by those supporting the church falls well short of a tithe or 10% of their income.

2) The figures given above exclude money given to non-Christian charitable organisations. The average person's disposable income is much higher than implied by the above figures; it is very likely that many Christian people do support non-Christian organisations. Maybe we need to teach church people to rethink the strategy they adopt for charitable giving. Non-Christian charities can appeal to the whole of the population of the United Kingdom, whereas the bulk of Christian organisations will get their support only from committed Christians. Should we encourage Christian people to give more specifically to Christian organisations

and attempt to help them formulate a strategy of giving?
3) These amounts of money are not large and few Christian organisations are wealthy. Should we seriously
contemplate widening the support base for Christian
organisations? There are some Christian businesses in
this country and there are many Christian Trusts, although the latter are frequently besieged by requests for
help. There are many secular businesses in which Christians work; could they be encouraged to ask their
companies to apply some of their social money to
Christian work? (Though companies with charitable
accounts are also besieged with requests.) We do not
know whether all church members actually do support
their local church, but it is likely that nominal church
members give less than church attenders. Should
greater attention be given to seeking to win nominal
members back into the fold (primarily for their salvation not for their money!), although with the recognition that if they do return to the church many will be
more likely to give more?

10: MISSIONARY AWARENESS

What of mission? Many factors affect the opportunity of
missionaries to work overseas today – the need for evangelism to the unreached, to nominal Christians, and those who
are effectively post-Christian. Poverty, injustice, urbanisation, an ageing population, and societal disintegration are
other factors. The growth of the church and the growth of
non-Christian religions are challenges in different ways. At
home, the local church competes with missionary interest. In
colleges, there are an increasing number of married students
in training, with a rising cost of accommodation and tuition at
theological colleges and Bible schools. There are declining
numbers of career missionaries. The image of societies is
questioned by some, with queries about their sometimes poor
communications; some ask if there are now too many societies, especially now that they face competition from relief

and development organisations, not helped as many have an ageing supporter base.

The overall numbers of Protestant missionaries are given below, quoting from the *UK Christian Handbook*. Catholic figures have not been collected for such a long period and so are shown to a different time scale in Table 13.

Table 12: Protestant missionaries 1972–2000

	Numbers 1972	Net change between 1972 and 1986	Numbers 1986	Net change between 1986 and 2000	Estimated numbers in 2000
Career missionaries	5,500	−1,600	3,900	−1,400	2,500
Short-term missionaries	700	+600	1,300	+300	1,600
Executive staff at home	800	−300	500	−100	400
Total missionary staff	7,000	−1,300	5,700	−1,200	4,500
Associates abroad	500	−300	200	+200	400
Office staff at home	700	+200	900	−250	650
Retired personnel at home	1,100	+100	1,200	+350	1,550
Total personnel	9,300	−1,300	8,000	−900	7,100

Table 12 shows a declining number of career missionaries, but an increasing number of short-termers. This trend is set to continue into the 1990s. This is partly because of the political uncertainties of the missionary operation; growth of churches in many lands overseas; growing numbers of missionaries from elsewhere. It is also partly because of the concern of missionaries for the education of their own children.[48] But short-term missionaries are not only finding out something of the thrill of cross-cultural evangelism, learning for themselves at square one, but frequently coming back for more!

Roman Catholic missionary numbers are given below.

Table 13: Catholic missionaries 1982–1994

	Numbers 1982	Net change between 1982 and 1988	Numbers 1988	Estimated net change between 1988 and 1994	Estimated numbers in 1994
Career missionaries	1,000	+130	1,130	+80	1,210
Short-term missionaries	370	−120	250	+20	270
Executive staff at home	410	−70	340	−40	300
Total missionary staff	1,780	−60	1,720	+60	1,780
Associates abroad	40	+20	60	0	60
Office staff at home	60	+20	80	+30	110
Retired personnel	70	+180	250	+80	330
Total personnel	1,950	+160	2,110	+170	2,280

Table 13 shows that although the number of Catholic missionaries might be much the same in 1994 as they were in 1982, the number of career missionaries will have increased by more than 20%. Executive staff at home would however decline. The number of retired personnel would however increase nearly five-fold over the same period. The Catholic missionary situation is therefore likely to become more active overseas, but with a larger number needing support at home after their years of service have been completed.

Where do we go from here? The Church is growing around

the world. In Britain our culture is changing, our church membership and church attendance are both growing though adversely affected by the number of elderly members who die. Nominal Christianity is declining, but our church congregations are increasing, though not always cohesively. Most churches tend to be small but, small or large, many – perhaps one in every five – have seen significant growth over the last few years. Currently there is a shortage of full-time ordained people available to meet the many openings, be these in this land or overseas, yet financial support is increasing, though not as fast as many would wish. What then is our vision? We have looked at its context. We are getting close to the need to 'write the vision; make it plain . . . so he may run who reads it'.[49] First though let us look at what the Scriptures say about this subject.

3: VISION AND THE SCRIPTURES

It was a night like any other. It grew dark and he went to bed. He drifted off to sleep, perhaps started snoring. Despite the hectic events of the days before he slept well. As Winston Churchill said of the night in May 1940 when King George VI asked him to form a government: 'Although impatient for the morning, I slept soundly, and had no need for cheering dreams. Facts are better than dreams.'[1]

Forty centuries ago, in what today is Southern Israel, Abram had tackled the army of four kings who had kidnapped his cousin Lot. Abram had rescued him. Melchizedek, the King of Salem, then met him on his return and blessed God for Abram's victory. Abram gave him a tenth of his spoil, and slept well that night.

Then it happened: the call of God in the night. Abram had heard God call before when he lived in Ur, so the experience was not new to him. Even so, Abram was worried. He didn't show it but God knew. Rescuing Lot was fine; he actually looked after his own kith and kin, but what of the promise to him as an individual? Where was his own child?

'Crawl out of your tent, Abram,' God said. So he did because he was obedient to God even when He asked unlikely things. 'Look at the stars,' God asked. 'How many do you see?'

In the clear skies of Hebron, the pinpoints of a million stars twinkled and beckoned to Abram, their sheer expanse and enormity gripping him. 'How many?' Abram could not answer. Today's astronomers estimate that with the naked eye you can see perhaps 2,000 stars and with a small telescope perhaps 10,000 – a minute fraction of the estimated 100 million billion billion (10^{26}). Like the apostle John who asked in his later vision of heaven where all those in white robes come from, Abram replied, 'Sir, you know'.

Then God spoke. 'That's how many children you will have.' Abram believed what God said, and the Lord credited that belief as righteousness. That step made Abram the 'Friend of God', with whom God shared His plans, and to whom Abram pleaded later for Sodom and Gomorrah. Ultimately God's promise was fulfilled beyond expectation when, as the Epistle to the Hebrews reminds us, he received Isaac 'as it were, back from the dead'.

This was a vision from God. Note that the vision came first and then the faith to believe in it. This vision encapsulated a promise which is being worked out even today. How typical was it? In this chapter we look at the biblical evidence for vision. This is crucial because the Bible is the foundation document not only for our church life, but for much of Western society even today.

DESCRIBING VISIONS

What are visions like? Who typically receives a vision? What is the difference between a 'vision' and a 'dream'? We can suggest several characteristics.

Visions are given to key people

Visions enable individual people to grasp something of God's over-arching plans for His kingdom in the human world and to take decisive action at critical points. So it was with Abram. He trusted God and though Ishmael was born, the patient wait for fulfilment was eventually rewarded with Isaac's birth. Now with a third of the world's five and a half billion people accepting the name of Christ there has been an enormous fulfilment, closer to Abram's original vision of the stars than he could have ever imagined.

What the Scriptures call 'visions' are invariably given to

important individuals and to them alone, even if they were
not alone at the time. In the Old Testament they were always
so given, and, as it happened, always to men. Women have
visions in the New Testament, as we shall see later.

So God speaks to Jacob and tells him to go down to Egypt.
God calls the boy Samuel and gives him dramatic news. Even
Nebuchadnezzar's dramatic vision of a huge but vulnerable
statue was made only to him. Nathan's vision was to him
alone, but his task was to communicate it to David. Likewise
Ahijah when he told Jeroboam he would be King of Israel,
and Zechariah as he counselled Uzziah.[2]

The New Testament also records key figures who had
visions. Among many examples, we can quote Zechariah
in the temple, Ananias and Paul separately in Damascus as
Paul's blindness goes as Ananias lays his hands on him,
Cornelius in Caesarea and Peter challenged at Joppa to
preach to Gentiles also, Paul at Troas and Corinth looking for
guidance, and John on Patmos Island as he worshipped. All
these had individual experiences. So did Paul when he was
'caught up to the third heaven'.[3] But the New Testament also
hints that visions may sometimes be seen collectively. Luke
uses the word to describe what the two women saw at the
empty tomb, and Matthew (alone of the Synoptic writers)
talks of the transfiguration as a vision which Peter, James and
John all experienced. These instances suggest that visions
may be shared, and may come to women as well as to men.

These special instances apart, the thrust of the Scriptures is
undoubtedly that visions are seen by influential people who
are given a dramatic and definite awareness. So today perhaps we should expect some people to receive a unique
revelation from the Lord. Certainly there could be dangers in
such visions since everyone's vision can only be a small part of
God's whole purpose. Nevertheless, vision prompting action
has frequently been significant for many people.

Visions involve participation with God

These individual encounters with God did not inhibit conversation. Abram asks the Lord a highly important question;

Jacob replies, 'Here I am'; Samuel tells God 'your servant is listening'; and Daniel asks, 'How can I, your servant, talk with you, my Lord? My strength is gone'. Zechariah replies to the angel; Ananias points out how dangerous a man Paul is; Cornelius asks what the Lord wanted; Peter declares his ritualistic purity; and John occasionally speaks with the angel.[4] The vision in no way prevents the individual from expressing his personality. Those who see visions are not under a hypnotic trance; they are aware, alive, and conscious of what is happening. God enables us to accommodate His presence with sanity and integrity.

Many of the visions in Scripture read like a play, with the action unfolding step by step. Daniel expressly uses the term 'watching the vision'. Jesus asked the three with him on the mountain not to 'tell anyone what you have *seen*'. John writes of what he 'saw in his vision'.[5]

This watching contrasts with the observer's physical movement. Peter was led out of prison by the angel and it was not until he was alone in Jerusalem's streets in the middle of the night that he suddenly understood that it was for real and *not* a vision. But though the vision might be something to watch, it did not prevent personal understanding of the event by the process of conversation.

Visions are stronger than dreams

God once gave to Moses, Miriam and Aaron the sign of a true prophet – 'I reveal myself to him in visions, I speak to him in dreams' (Numbers 12:6, NIV). This Hebrew parallelism shows that visions and dreams are close but nevertheless distinct. Similarly, Joel's words (2:28, NIV), quoted on the Day of Pentecost, give another parallelism:

> Your sons and daughters will prophesy,
> Your old men will dream dreams
> Your young men will see visions.

This sense of the ordinary as well as the special is reflected in the word 'see' which here (and in Numbers 24:4,16 with

Balak, NIV) is the usual word for seeing or beholding, looking upon or appearing. The same is true in the New Testament quotation of this verse. It is not the usual word for seeing a vision which derives from the word for 'seer'. Daniel (1:17) was given the gift of understanding 'visions and dreams of all kinds'.

What then is the meaning of the word 'vision'? In the Hebrew various words are used all associated with the same notation (transliterated as Chazoth, Chazuth, Chezer, Chizzayon, Machazeh) all of which are overwhelmingly translated only as 'vision' in the Authorised Version (AV). The essential meaning of the word is 'to see, behold, look at, gaze upon, perceive' and perhaps through the last of these, 'to feel, or to experience'. There is an element of alert awareness, a deliberate consciousness. In Greek the key word used is ὃραμα, meaning 'that which is seen': a sight or a spectacle which is to be watched.

That visions and dreams are similar is reinforced by Job 4:13. Translated as 'amid disquieting dreams in the night' in the New International Version (NIV) translation, the actual Hebrew word is that used almost exclusively for 'vision'. More parallels occur in Job 7:14, 20:8, 33:15 and Isaiah 29:7. In the New Testament Peter describes his experience to the apostles – 'in a trance I saw a vision'. Visions are stronger than dreams, reflected in the title of Jacqueline Buskin's book (Pan, 1987), *Dreams are not enough*.

What then are some of the differences?

Dreams are:	*Visions are:*
Had	Seen
Frequent	Rare
Natural	Special
Sometimes symbolic	Clear
Transient	Permanent
Remembered	Followed
Personal	For sharing
Often past or present orientated	Future orientated
Often preparation for action	For action
Often about imaginary events	Predictions of real events
Given to everybody	Given to influencers/leaders

Visions are detailed

The clarity of the detail in a vision is normally special. Ezekiel minutely described the New Jerusalem. He could easily see the idolatrous writing on the walls deep within the Temple. Daniel observed the visions that came with such exactitude that he was overcome by the symbolism they represented. Nathan described the future of God's blessing to David and his line in clear qualitative terms, so that David was able to respond in a deep and wonderful prayer of worship. The New Testament visions likewise are extremely clear. Peter could see exactly the types of animals in the sheet; John was able to view the vast panorama of the future in such detail that sometimes the angels told him not to write it down.[6]

The visions of Ezekiel and Daniel especially show far greater detail than could possibly otherwise be known. The Israelite elders must have been greatly embarrassed by Ezekiel's minute descriptions of their actions, not least when they were actually named. Likewise, Ezekiel's description of the New Jerusalem is masterly in its exactness. The life of Daniel and his friends depended on the detail of Nebuchad-nezzar's dream being shown to them, and subsequently Daniel's visions had the same qualities, indeed so much so that he was appalled by them and became physically ill.[7]

Visions are often associated with physical elements

Some visions have external visual stimuli. Abram's vision concerned the stars and the Lord actually drew him to a physical appreciation of their magnitude, not just recalling in his memory what they looked like, as would have happened in a dream.

Sometimes the visual effects were so startling, as with Ezekiel, that it is difficult to know exactly how external they were. Ezekiel describes his vision of the Lord of the Wheels in terms he would probably have used were he describing an event he was watching rather than one which he dreamt – the windstorm, the sound of their wings, the standing on his feet,

and the eating of the scroll for example. Ezekiel's other
visions are similar. 'The Spirit lifted me up between earth and
heaven and in visions of God took me to Jerusalem' and later
'brought me to the exiles in Babylonia'.[8] His later vision of
the New Jerusalem in Chapter 40 is also similar.

The transfiguration vision on the mount was obviously
almost entirely external to the three disciples. Paul was led
away blind on the Damascus Road. Peter's watching the
descending sheet in the house in Joppa had the corroboration
of three strangers knocking on the door. Zechariah was
struck dumb as he ministered in the temple. This kind of
physical consequence is not only visible in the New Testament. Isaiah experienced a burning coal cleansing his lips.
Ezekiel and Daniel were both told to stand up, even though
Daniel found it very difficult – he preferred to stay on his
hands and knees. In confirmation of what Ezekiel had seen,
Pelatiah, son of Benaiah, fell down dead as he was describing
his vision to the leaders of the people. Ezekiel, as John later,
ate the scroll offered to him, it tasting like honey in his
mouth.[9]

The effect of such external events would ensure that the
recipients would not forget what they had seen, and, more
importantly, from whom the vision had come.

Visions are the word of the Lord

In many visions there is a clear link with the divine originator.
It was the 'word of the Lord' which came to Abram, the Lord
calling Samuel because the 'word of the Lord was rare'.
'The word of the Lord came to Ezekiel the priest' and to
Nathan. Isaiah quoted 'what the Lord says to me'. It was God
who spoke, 'This is my Son, whom I love' at the transfigur-
ation, and 'the Lord (who) spoke to Paul in a vision' in
Corinth.[10]

It is God's authentic voice which is heard in visions, which
is why the false prophets were so condemned. God's revela-
tory authority is at stake, and in the transmission of truth He
brooks no unauthorised channels. This is the Sovereign God
who is speaking. Let the earth tremble and disobey if it dare.

God is the source; the responsibility of transmission is His. God's recipients, who would become His mouthpieces, were very sure of the divine presence on those occasions, and sometimes especially of the Spirit Himself. So today no vision can be true if it is not in accord with the written word of the Lord, however His Spirit may show it to His servants.

The link of the Spirit of the Lord with a vision to His servant is particularly prominent in Ezekiel, where the Scriptures record on several occasions, 'The Spirit lifted me up' or 'The Spirit of the Lord came upon me'. Joel also indicates that it is after the Lord has poured out 'my Spirit on all people' that 'your young men will see visions'. And it was 'while Peter was still thinking about the vision, (that) the Spirit' spoke to him.[11] All visions come through the power of the Holy Spirit. Without Him, nothing is given.

WHAT CHARACTERISES A VISION?

Visions can come at any time

Abram's vision came at night so that the Lord could show him the stars. Daniel was lying in his bed at night when at least one of his visions came to him, and Nebuchadnezzar's vision came in the same way. Samuel was also lying down in the temple, with 'the lamp of God not yet gone out' when the Lord called him. The word of God came to Nathan at night. Paul had his Macedonian vision 'during the night', as did his affirmation to stay on in Corinth.[12]

Ezekiel on the other hand had his vision 'while I was among the exiles by the Kebar River', which could refer to his physical location during the day. Daniel had one of his visions 'standing on the bank of the great river, the Tigris'.

Cornelius had his vision at three o'clock in the afternoon, and the following day Peter had his 'about noon'. The transfiguration took place during the day, as did Paul's conversion experience en route to Damascus (which he calls a vision). Zechariah had his in the day-time while burning the incense in the temple. The women at the tomb saw the angels early on a Sunday morning (which Luke describes as a vision).[13]

Visions seem to be able to be given at any time, night or day, depending on the outward circumstances of the person, their potential receptivity and an appropriate place for the vision itself. God gives visions when people are able to see them, and this may be when there are fewest distractions – hence at night, or unexpectedly during the day in a major and unmistakable special event.

God's timing is always right. Sometimes the exact hour is important, as with Peter on the rooftop. It was just as the vision finished, that the folk from Caesarea knocked on his door. Peter said it was 'right then' when describing it to his brother apostles. Ananias had a vision at the same time, or perhaps just shortly after Paul had one. Nathan's vision came the night after David decided to build the temple. Habakkuk's came after he decided to wait and see 'what answer I am to give to this complaint', Isaiah had a very real sense of timing at the end of his vision when he asked 'For how long, O Lord?'[14] God's clocks are precise!

Visions invariably come unexpectedly. Only Daniel is recorded as deliberately seeking them, once to save the lives of himself and his three friends, and once when he determined to try and understand what he had already seen. For all the ones recorded in Scripture, visions came unexpectedly. Abram did not know what God would do, when he woke him that night four thousand years ago. Samuel did not expect God to meet with him as he willingly served in the Temple; indeed in those days 'there were not many visions'. The prophets might have come to expect visions after seeing several, but initially they just came at God's appointed moment. As Amos answered Amaziah, 'I was neither a prophet nor a prophet's son, but I was a shepherd . . . and the Lord said to me "Go, prophesy"'. As God's call is unanticipated, so are visions. Hence the surprise of Zechariah when Gabriel spoke to him, and Cornelius.[15] Ananias could not have known that he would have a vision the night Paul reached Damascus, nor did Paul when he sought his next destination. Thus visions come when a Sovereign Lord desires. While we of course cannot force them out of Him, we should not be frightened if He should choose to show one to us today.

Visions are transforming and irreversible

Apart perhaps from the prophets like Ezekiel, who seemed to have had many visions, visions happen rarely. Abram is recorded as having only one, and so are many others – Jacob, Peter, Nathan and so on. Paul refers to having had one 'fourteen years ago' (2 Corinthians 12:2). There is only the transfiguration which is recorded as a vision in the whole three years of Jesus' ministry. Visions are special and important events.

Paul describes his as having been taken up to the 'third heaven', or 'was caught up to Paradise'. Ezekiel is frequently caught up by the Spirit of God. John knew he was 'in heaven'. Paul was uncertain whether he was in his body or not.[16]

Some visions are 'inexpressible' (2 Corinthians 12:4). In others the recipient is not permitted to tell, indicating that the effect of the vision, or that part of it, is solely for their edification.

Visions cannot be undone, nor can the message be altered once delivered. Ezekiel could say quite definitely 'the seller will not recover the land he has sold . . . Because of their sins, not one of them shall preserve his life' (7:13). Zechariah was dumb until his son John was born and circumcised. Visions are not jokes or transitory affairs soon to be forgotten. God is serious in His communications, and does not intend us to forget them, or think they will not come true. God is working out His Sovereign purposes, and permits some of His servants sometimes to see part of what is to happen. Let no one think the outworking will not happen.

WHO RECEIVES VISIONS?

Prophets as part of their prophetic profession

A prophet is more than one who proclaims the future; he or she applies the principles of God's kingdom to the present. He or she needs to be intimate with God; part of such intimacy can come through visions. Thus Isaiah can describe his whole book as 'the vision concerning Judah and Jerusalem that Isaiah son of Amoz saw'. The Chronicler describes how Hezekiah's 'acts of devotion are written in the vision of the prophet Isaiah'. Daniel receives the answer to Nebuchadnezzar's impossible request of someone else describing to him his dream 'during the night . . . in a vision', but made it clear to that monarch that the source was the 'God in heaven who reveals mysteries'.[17]

When 'calamity upon calamity will come and rumour upon rumour', people 'will try and get a vision from the prophet' (Ezekiel 7:26, NIV). This desperate turning to the representative of the Lord, to try and force him to do his job, underwrites the expectation that a prophet will normally see visions. So should their contemporary parallels today. Uzziah is reported as seeking God 'during the days of Zechariah, who instructed him in the fear (vision) of God' (2 Chronicles 26:5, NIV) as if this teaching programme were an accepted part of the prophet's task. Solomon's reign is described earlier in 2 Chronicles as being written 'in the records of Nathan the prophet, and in the vision of Iddo the seer', with the only vision Nathan recorded as receiving being that given to prevent David personally building the temple.[18] Thus even if this was the only vision Nathan received it is not only not assumed to be incongruous with his prophetic profession but part of it.

Receiving a vision authenticates a prophet. Hosea says God 'spoke to prophets (and) gave them many visions'. Obadiah and Nahum state their message is their vision. Nebuchadnezzar expected Daniel to be able to interpret his visions. The clearest description of the prophetic vision comes when the Lord addresses Miriam and Aaron, 'when a prophet of the Lord is among you, I reveal myself to him in visions' and goes on to indicate His special relationship with Moses with whom He speaks 'mouth to mouth, clearly, and not in dark speech'.[19]

Should we not expect present-day prophets likewise to have visions from the Lord? Although not a prophet, Balaam acts in the same way before King Balak as he professes to give 'the oracle of one who hears the words of God . . . who sees a vision from the Almighty'. He recognises that a revelation

must come from God if it is to be authentic. Peter never
questioned the authenticity of his revelation, knowing it came
from God ('Surely not, *Lord!*'[20]) even though he too was not
a prophet. The book of Revelation is undoubtedly a vision
even though John calls it such only once. He does refer to it
also as a prophecy at the beginning and end of his book,
without any sense of incongruity.[21] The prophetic vocation is
certainly authenticated by seeing visions, but it is not dependent upon them. Nor does the vision make the prophet, so the
exceptional few who receive a single vision from the Lord are
not necessarily made prophets thereby.

When Israel and Judah fell from following the Lord, part of
their punishment was that 'her king and her princes are exiled
among the nations . . . and her prophets no longer find
visions from the Lord'. Whether the exiles 'listen or fail to
listen . . . they will know a prophet has been among them'
when Ezekiel describes his visionary message.[22]

The Scriptures condemn those who claim to speak on
behalf of the Lord when they have no direct word from Him.
But false prophets realised that as true prophets had visions,
so they too needed to speak as if they had had a vision.
Jeremiah roundly condemns all such when he repeats 'What
the Lord Almighty says: "Do not listen to what the prophets
are prophesying to you. They speak visions from their own
minds"' (23:16). Clearly therefore visions can be imagined,
an event readily acknowledged by leaders today.[23]

As a consequence of 'the prophets (leading) my people
astray . . . night will come over you, without visions' (Micah
3:5, 6). False prophets mean the absence of true vision.

False prophets will be punished. 'On that day . . . I will
remove both the prophets and the spirit of impurity from the
land'. As a consequence, 'on that day every prophet will be
ashamed of his prophetic vision'.[24] False prophets *know* they
are being false.

Part of the hope for the future is that 'there will be no more
false visions'. The perpetrators of such visions are to be
condemned. In a chapter in which Ezekiel spells out the fate
of such prophets he describes their visions on six occasions.
Four times they are 'false', once they are 'lying' and once they

'saw visions of peace for (Jerusalem) when there was no peace'. These men prophesied 'out of their own imagination', followed 'their own spirit', 'have seen nothing'. They are 'like foxes among ruins'[25] who, being ravenous for food, become more and more unrestrained and crafty in their efforts to get it. 'They were like plaster, concealing the crumbling structure of the nation, but unable to stop it falling'.[26] They would therefore be completely and violently punished without remedy, because 'they put a reproach upon divine revelation, lessen its credit, and weaken its credibility'.[27]

Other passages likewise condemn the wicked prophets. Invariably the word used in conjunction with the wrongness of their visions is 'false'. The effect is likened to divination. It is clear that such false visions originate from those speaking 'from their own minds, not from the mouth of the Lord',[28] thus generating false hopes in their listeners. Their messages are self-generated, reflecting the energy of the flesh, not the Spirit. Because visions exercise such a crucial role in stimulating leadership, it is essential they are divinely originated. So the basic principle of leading, 'checking your signals' as Tom Sine puts it,[29] is invalidated by these men who are more anxious for themselves than their message. Such tendencies and temptations are with us today, and we need therefore to 'test the Spirit' of the seers who see modern-day visions. It is not what the audience wishes to learn, but what God has to show that is essential.

No one: there is no vision!

The absence of vision may also come from the abuse of the office of prophet. 'Priests and prophets stagger from beer and are befuddled with wine; . . . they stagger when seeing visions, they stumble when rendering decisions' (Isaiah 28:7, NIV). Drunken prophets not only lose one key element of their vocation, but make mistakes in their leadership of the nation.

Sometimes the vision is correctly given but the interpretation is hidden from the recipients. 'Be stunned and amazed, . . . be drunk but not from wine . . . the Lord has brought

over you a deep sleep: He has sealed your eyes (the prophets)
. . . For you this whole vision is nothing but words sealed in a
scroll' (Isaiah 29:9–11). Thus the meaning of the vision is as
imperative as the vision itself. They are not given for the
prophets' amusement, but for the people's education.

Sometimes the meaning of the vision is given to the prophet
and he is either told not to repeat it, or he keeps it to himself.
Thus Daniel found his visions deeply troubling and conse-
quently 'kept the matter to myself'. Gabriel told him to 'seal
up the (next) vision, for it concerns the distant future', and
later to 'seal the words of the scroll until the time of the end'.
John was told, 'seal up what the seven thunders have said and
do not write it down'.

The purpose of secrecy is partly because it is beyond the
understanding of those who would be told. It relates to the
future. 'The vision awaits its time; it hastens to the end . . . it
will surely come, it will not delay'. It seems the concealment
comes primarily from the time lapse between the revelation
and its fulfilment rather than because the hearers' hearts are
'calloused'. On the other hand, Isaiah's vision was to preach
to the nation 'lest they might see with their eyes, hear with
their ears . . . and turn and be healed'.[30]

Other people

Visions are never given for an individual's private benefit.
Abram's which might seem an exception, was given not only
that he could know the answer to an intimate problem but
also to defer him from taking the legal action which would
have made Eliezer his heir. Paul's vision of the Macedonian
man was to guide him and his party across Europe. His vision
while he was at Corinth was to reassure him that the Lord had
many people in that city.[31]

The visions given to the prophets were invariably related
either to their people and country in general, or to the kings,
priests and other leaders in particular. Isaiah's vision concerned 'Judah and Jerusalem', and the Lord bid him 'Go and
tell *this people*'.[32] Ezekiel's visions repeatedly allowed him to
watch the private actions of the country's leaders which he

subsequently denounced. While Daniel's visions partly related directly to Nebuchadnezzar, most seemingly were given so that they could be recorded in writing since they concerned the 'time of the end' or 'a time yet to come', rather than for him to tell his fellow citizens. Indeed once Daniel had recovered from the exhaustion which followed the vision, he went about his normal business.[33]

Sometimes the word 'vision' is used in conjunction with Israel's enemies, as when Isaiah had 'a dire vision' concerning the Fall of Babylon (21:2, 9).

Other people who received visions also had them to help another person. Nathan's was to correct King David's action; Samuel's was to warn Eli, Ananias' was to persuade him to help Paul, and Peter's persuaded him to go to Cornelius.[34]

So visions can be given to concerned or willing recipients who will act on what they see. Courage and grace so to do is given by the Lord, just as He sends His angels to strengthen the recipients when required to receive the vision in the first place. They are not given for casual or private enjoyment, as dreams may be. The conditions for participation are quite different from receiving or experiencing the gift of speaking in tongues, for instance. The sequence in Daniel Chapter 9 is illuminating. Daniel was reading and pondering the Scriptures and 'understood . . . that the desolation of Jerusalem would last seventy years'. So he 'turned to the Lord God and pleaded with him in prayer and petition, in fasting and in sackcloth and ashes'. While he 'was still in prayer, Gabriel . . . came to' him (9:2, 3 and 21). Who then is troubled deeply enough about God's work in this world so to pray as Daniel did? God may bestow the gift of vision to such people.

To young men?

The precise age at which most of these who received visions in Scripture is not usually stated. Abram was between 76 and 80, and Jacob was perhaps a year short of the 130 he mentioned to Pharaoh to allow time for the journey from Canaan.[35] The exactness of these two is the exception. One may presume that most of the prophets were middle-aged men. David's desire to build the temple came towards the end of his forty-year reign. Nathan was presumably an old man, like his master, when he received his vision. Peter and Paul were perhaps in their thirties when the experiences at Joppa and the Damascus Road took place. The apostle John was an old man when he saw the revelation. If one had to weigh up the biblical evidence such as it is, one would say that visions tend to be given to men mature in their life, at middle-age or older, sometimes when they were very old. Only Samuel is recorded as having a vision when he was a boy in the temple.

So the reference in Joel is therefore especially curious. He writes (2:28):

> I will pour out my Spirit on all people,
> Your sons and daughters will prophesy,
> Your old men will dream dreams,
> Your young men will see visions.

This verse suggests, if taken literally, that it is the young people rather than senior citizens who can expect to see visions, and indeed emphasises the fact by contrasting the two. Matthew Henry thinks that men of both age groups will both dream dreams and see visions, the old to have their spirits reinvigorated and the young to have experiences of divine things. This is not the view of Jamieson, Fausset and Brown who feel visions are specially referred to young men, 'as adapted to their more lively minds'.[36] Others consider it is the universality of the outpouring of God's Spirit that is here in view, regardless of age, sex or class, emphasised by the statement that the outpouring will be on '*all* people'. It is in this light that Peter applies it on the day of Pentecost; 'this is what was spoken by the prophet Joel . . . let *all* Israel be assured . . . repent, every one of you'.[37]

The image of 'pouring out' in the above verse suggests the symbol of water, of a mighty rolling stream. The Holy Spirit will come upon all, irrespective of race, sex, background or location. In the immediate context of Joel this would include the Gentiles. In the context of Acts it was to open the gates to all who would repent and receive the gift of the Holy Spirit. It is receptivity rather than physical or social conditions that allow dreams to be dreamed and visions to be seen. How receptive are we? How receptive are young people? Samuel was an authoritative leader, influenced for his entire life by that night in which the certainty of the Lord's presence and purpose became particularly personal. How many more outstanding Christian leaders might there be if indeed it was the 'young men' (and young women) who saw visions?

WHY DO VISIONS COME?

Visions always seek to help the kingdom of God forward. God never gives visions gratuitously. Visions are essential for direction, control and encouragement. But they are not generated by humankind, but rather are bestowed by God. Visions seem to be given for one or more of the following reasons:

Visions enlarge our understanding of current events

Interpreting the present was part of the work of each of the prophets. Isaiah's vision extended over four reigns and was to continue 'until the Lord has sent everyone far away'. To understand his task better, God met with him in a vision. Ezekiel saw what the elders of Israel were actually doing, and thus could prophesy more precisely. Peter's vision helped him realise the Gospel was for the Gentiles also. Paul's vision of the Macedonian man came after fruitless endeavours to go elsewhere, and directed him to a new continent. The transfiguration confirmed to the three disciples that Jesus really was the Lord God.[38]

Visions show the promised future

Abram could be assured that God would keep his promise, even if it took many years. As an old man seeking a wife for his son Isaac, he was certain God would 'send his angel before' his servant. Jacob also was assured that the move to Egypt was in line with God's promise and that the promise to

Abram of migration to a foreign land was about to happen. Because Eli's sons treated 'the Lord's offering with contempt', he was told that the punishment 'there would never be an old man in your family line' was about to happen. Some taunted Ezekiel by saying, 'The vision he sees is for many years from now', but the Lord replied, 'None of my words will be delayed any longer'. The expectation is that a vision will be fulfilled, so the Sovereign Lord tells Ezekiel, 'The days are near when every vision will be fulfilled'. There is despair and disbelief if they are not seen to come true, but fulfilling a vision strengthened hope and trust. Ezekiel prophesied firmly that the proud, impregnable Tyre would one day vanish, so there was great rejoicing when the city was finally destroyed. Habakkuk was assured 'the vision awaits an appointed time'. Daniel was told, 'The saints of the Most High will receive the kingdom and will possess it for ever'. John heard the saints sing 'they will reign on the earth'.[39]

Visions give immediate guidance

God did not intend that the warrior King David should build the temple, though the thought in David's heart was perfectly acceptable: peaceful Solomon should build it instead. This was why Nathan had a vision the night after David announced his plans. Paul was not to travel into Europe but to stay in Corinth. He could later say to King Agrippa, 'I was not disobedient to the vision from heaven'. Zechariah was about to have a son who was to be called John. Cornelius was to send some men to Joppa. There were times when Ezekiel was specially commanded to prophesy, and often the Spirit of the Lord would come upon him. Such guidance was given when God's servants were genuinely perplexed – where should Paul go next? What was to happen to Abram's inheritance? Dare Jacob go out of the promised land? Deep problems are part of the pathway God sets for us; visions are one of the ways He uses to answer our unarticulated queries. Just as we 'do not know what we ought to pray' and 'the Spirit himself intercedes for us' so 'he who searches our hearts' sometimes leads us definitely and dramatically through a vision.[40]

Visions give encouragement

After his vision, Abram realised God was working for many generations to come and could comfort himself with the thought that his own interests were protected. Paul was encouraged to stay in Corinth as the Lord had 'many people in this city'. Ezekiel was 'to pay attention to everything (the Lord was) going to show' him, so that he could 'tell the House of Israel everything'. The House of Israel, absorbed by the vision of the New Jerusalem, would be encouraged and challenged 'never again (to) defile my holy name'. David was assured that 'one of your own sons . . . will build a house'. Paul was caught up to the third heaven, and was 'given a thorn in (his) flesh' 'to keep (him) from becoming conceited because of these surpassingly great revelations'.[41]

Visions are a response to prayer

It is surely no accident that when Zechariah received his vision Gabriel assured him, 'your prayer has been heard'. So had those of Cornelius. It was while Daniel 'was speaking and praying, confessing my sin and the sin of my people Israel' that Gabriel came to 'give (him) insight and understanding'. He said, 'As soon as you began to pray, an answer was given, which I have come to tell you'. The Lord graciously encourages His people, sometimes even with a vision, to assure us that our prayers are heard. No wonder Jesus told His disciples, 'Ask and you will receive, and your joy will be complete.'[42]

Donald Bridge in his book *When Christians Doubt* (MARC, 1988) focuses on the experience of Job. Of all people, one could have expected Job to wither under the deluge of disasters that happened to him and his family. But he didn't and the biblical record shows how his faith stays firm most of the time. At the end God reveals Himself, and without answering the fundamental question of why He had allowed Job to suffer so much, gives Job a vision. Job's response was 'I spoke of things I did not understand. My ears had heard of you but *now my eyes have seen you*'.[43] This vision of God (a) highlights Job's limited viewpoint as he is confined to one point of time and space, (b) reinforces that God is in control of all events however strange they may be, and (c) acknowledges the seen and the unseen, the explicable and the inexplicable, in every event.

THE EFFECT OF VISIONS

Understanding

The prophet was expected to make the vision clear. Habakkuk was expressly told to 'Write the vision; make it plain upon tablets, so he may see who reads it', that is, take appropriate action. Peter wondered about the explanation of his vision on the rooftop, but obeyed the Spirit when He told him to go with the men from Caesarea. Visions were not usually given solely for the recipient's knowledge, amusement or private stimulation. Paul's visit to the 'third heaven' is perhaps the exception that proves the rule. But the visionary or the dreamer must never become so carried away by seeing his prophecies fulfilled that he causes people to slip away from their love of the Lord. Moses was adamant – if a man so acted he was not to be followed; God was testing his people's understanding.[44]

Praise

David's heartfelt ambition was to build something great and distinctive for the Lord. He was essentially loyal to God, even if his actions were sometimes well out of tune. His dream of a temple came from contrasting his own position after his victories and the state of the Ark. 'Here I am, living in a palace of cedar, while the ark of God remains in a tent.' What then will he do when God refuses him his desire through a vision to Nathan? He praises God in a soaring psalm of thanks. 'Give thanks to the Lord . . . sing praise to him . . . glory in his holy name . . . For great is the Lord and most worthy of praise.' The true response to what God reveals is captured by David. Unfortunately visions rarely seem to generate such thanks. However, Daniel did give thanks when God showed him Nebuchadnezzar's dream – 'Praise be to the name of God for ever and ever'. After discussing Peter's vision and the events in Caesarea, the Apostles eventually 'praised God, saying, "So then, God, has granted even the Gentiles repentance unto life"'.[45]

Obedience

When Jacob was assured that the Lord really wanted him to move to Egypt with all its implications for the sacred promises, he obeyed and went to meet Joseph. David desisted from building the temple but asked God to keep His word, 'And now, Lord, let the promise you have made . . . be established for ever'. Having received the vision, 'Ananias went to the house and (placed) his hands on Saul', though not without first querying the matter with the Lord. Cornelius sent his servants to Joppa, and Peter instantly went with them, 'the Spirit told me to have no hesitation'. 'After Paul had seen the (Macedonian) vision, we got ready at once to leave', showing not only Paul's immediate response but the trust of the other members of his party (including presumably Luke) as they prepared to go with him. Paul continued on in Corinth expressly because of his vision – '*So* Paul stayed for a year and half'. Paul's claim to King Agrippa, 'I was not disobedient to the heavenly vision' summarises what God expects when he gives a vision – attention and obedience. Visions are pragmatic directives.[46]

Trust

With obedience goes trust. David trusted God to work out this part of His promise with his descendants, something over which David had no ultimate control. Abram 'believed the Lord' that his offspring would be as many as the stars. Trust and acceptance are closely related. Samuel had the vision of judgment, and Eli accepted it, 'He is the Lord: let Him do what is good in His eyes'.[47]

Proclamation

As far as most major and minor prophets in the Old Testament were concerned, the purpose of the visions they were
given was simple – to pass the message on to the people of
Israel or Judah or the exiles in Babylon. 'Then the vision I had
seen went up from me,' wrote Ezekiel, 'and I told the exiles
everything the Lord had shown me.' This typical action could
be reflected by numerous other examples. One purpose of
such proclamation was to ensure obedience and give assurance and confidence to God's people.

In Daniel's book, Nebuchadnezzar had a vivid dream
which Daniel describes also as a vision. 'There is a God in
heaven who reveals mysteries. He has shown King
Nebuchadnezzar what will happen in days to come.' As
Daniel then unfolds the meaning, the purpose of his explanation becomes clearer. It was to show the potential God-
fearing King (a) the greatness of God's power, (b) the continuous nature of His rule, (c) the humble acknowledgment
He requires of His Sovereignty, and (d) the justice of His
ways. And what Daniel proclaims is ultimately borne out in
the King's personal and trying experience until he acknowledges that God is the universal ruler.[48]

Likewise in the New Testament, visions led to the proclamation of the good news. Cornelius was to 'send to Joppa
for Simon (who) will bring a message through which you and
all your household will be saved'. The Macedonian vision
meant that Paul's party concluded 'that God had called us to
preach the gospel to them'. God had many people in Corinth.
Paul's obedience to his heavenly vision meant he preached to
Jews and Gentiles that they should repent and turn to God.
Should such proclamations be expected from any who claim
modern-day visions? The answer must surely be 'yes'.[49]

These are positive reactions to visions: understanding,
praise, obedience, trust and proclamation. But negative reactions were also generated.

Negative reactions

The actual vision or its message often frightened the individual who received it. Samuel was 'afraid to tell Eli the vision'. Job was 'disquieted', frightened and even terrified by God's warnings. Daniel 'was greatly perplexed' until the King told him not to worry. The disciples on the Mount of Transfiguration 'fell face down to the ground, terrified'. Zechariah 'was gripped with fear'. The women at the resurrection tomb were frightened and uncertain.[50]

Daniel's 'thoughts alarmed him'; he 'was troubled in spirit', 'deeply troubled' so that his 'face turned pale'. 'So I was left alone, gazing at this great vision; I had no strength left, my face turned deathly pale and I was helpless'. He was 'overcome with anguish because of the vision'. 'My strength is gone and I can hardly breathe.' Clearly receiving visions can be devastating. Daniel's experience is echoed by Ezekiel's and Isaiah's. 'I sat among (the exiles) overwhelmed for seven days – and silent' said Ezekiel. 'My heart falters, fear makes me tremble' stated Isaiah.[51]

Sometimes the physical distress went further still. 'A dire vision has been shown to me . . . my body is racked with pain', Isaiah cried. Daniel 'lay ill for several days'. 'Fear and trembling seized me and made all my bones shake', said Job. Sometimes those accompanying the seer were affected, 'the men with (Daniel) did not see it, but such terror overwhelmed them that they fled and hid themselves'. 'The men travelling with Saul stood there speechless.'[52]

Why these reactions? Since these dramatic effects are confined to relatively few prophets and leaders the trouble is not universal. Perhaps it is because the meaning of the vision is as important as the vision itself. Hence Daniel's prayer for understanding and Gabriel's personal answer. 'Since the first day that you set your mind to gain understanding . . . your words were heard, and I have come in response.' When he 'heard, but . . . did not understand' he asked questions. Likewise Peter wondered 'about the meaning of the vision' and 'was still thinking' when the men from Cornelius arrived. The purposes of God need to be understood accurately. The principle is the same as with speaking in tongues – this is fine so long as there is an interpreter in a congregation.[53]

THE IMPORTANCE OF VISIONS

We have mostly thus far kept to the scriptural references where the word 'vision' is actually used. But with some events, clearly visions, the word is never actually used. Thus Isaiah's dramatic understanding of a Sovereign God in His Temple, with trembling foundations, is the key to his ministry, yet neither in Chapter 6, nor elsewhere in his book is any reference made to that event as a 'vision'. The insights of thundering Amos are never described as 'visions'. Ezekiel has many visions, and his challenge in Chapter 37 of dry bones coming together and forming a living people for the Lord has been helpful for many. Yet the word 'vision' does not occur in that chapter. Neither the colossal ark which Noah built, nor the Tabernacle of Moses are described as visions, despite the importance of both.

The Psalmist acknowledges the importance of visions. 'Once', he said, 'you spoke in a vision, to your faithful people' (89:19), concerning the designation of the young warrior David to be King. Most modern versions translate the Hebrew as indicating that this vision was communicated to the people as a whole (that is, 'your people' is taken in the plural) (so NIV, RV, GNB, NEB). Other versions take the vision as being given to a single individual. 'Your holy one' (so AV, RAV, RSV, Amplified). *The Jerusalem Bible* inserts the name of the persons as 'Samuel and Nathan' and the *Living Bible* as 'Samuel'. But however many receive the vision, the basic and fundamental importance of its occurrence and its transmission stands.

Isaiah refers in one chapter to the 'Valley of Vision' (22:1 and 5) that figurative place where the prophecies of the destruction of Jerusalem were to be fulfilled. 'The Lord Almighty has a day of tumult and trampling and terror in the Valley of Vision.' It is near Jerusalem because that was where God was known. Babylon, a stranger to God, was called 'the desert of the sea'.[54] The burden of this chapter is that Jerusalem will be frightened but not ruined, for it relates not to Nebuchadnezzar's sacking but the attempt made on it by Sennacherib. The importance of this 'oracle' is not only

Isaiah's concern to cause the people to repent of their sin and indifference but also that he speaks in the name of the Almighty God. In the New Testament particularly, the importance of some of the visions is emphasised by the fact that they were communicated directly by angels, even Gabriel, or one of the twenty-four elders.[55]

But perhaps the most well-known section of the Scriptures relating to the importance of visions is that which, in the Authorised Version, reads 'where there is no vision, the people perish' (Proverbs 29:18). The way other translations handle this verse is illuminating. 'Where there is no vision, the people get out of hand' (Jerusalem). 'Where there is no revelation, the people cast off restraint' (NIV). 'Where there is no prophecy, the people cast off restraint' (RSV). 'Where there is no one in authority, the people break loose' (NEB). 'A nation without God's guidance is a nation without order' (GNB).

Two of the alternative words used for vision – revelation, prophecy – are used elsewhere in the Scriptures to translate the same Hebrew word. The need for help, clear leadership, firm understanding comes through.

The Scriptures also show us the dramatic consequences of not having such leadership and understanding. A loose morality, an indifference to others, a loss of the essential order in society . . . they are all reflections of what it means to 'perish'. How are we to avoid twentieth-century parallels? The visions recorded in the Scriptures show God taking the initiative in communicating to people. Many times today men and women, praying for guidance and help, are prompted by the Spirit to say, write and proclaim those ideas which come with the force of some of the visions of old. How do we obtain a vision for ourselves, our church or organisation, even our country?

4: FINDING YOUR VISION

I don't always stop for hitch-hikers, but I did pick up one young man who turned out to be an agricultural engineering student in his final year. When I asked him about his career plans, he replied vaguely that he would 'get a job'. 'What kind of job?' 'One that involves my engineering qualification', was the answer. He could not find an answer at all when I pressed him to think about what he might be doing in ten years' time.

Similarly, a young woman came to MARC Europe one day for an interview and was asked what she would be doing in ten years' time. Her reply was, 'I hope to have learnt the basics of my profession, and to have started a family. When they're grown up then I can continue working'. A twenty-three year old applied to us for a key position. When she was asked what she would be doing by the time she was thirty-three, she replied without hesitation, 'I'll be in francophone Africa translating the Bible'.

What would you like to be doing in ten years' time? One of the leading leaders of life-work planning, John Crystal, says, 'You don't start out saying, "I need a job". You start by asking, "What do I want to do with my life?"' In John Naisbitt's second major book, *Re-inventing the Corporation*, he quotes Buck Blessing, a career consultant, who says, 'The most difficult person to manage is the person who has no idea what he or she wants to do'.

Anne Townsend in her book *Mid-life Crisis* tells the story of three workmen building St Paul's Cathedral. They were each asked what they were doing. The first looked fed up and said, 'I'm chipping this stone'. The second replied, 'I'm cutting this block to fit into that corner'. The third lifted his head high with dignity and stated, 'I'm helping Sir Christopher Wren build a Cathedral!'

What sort of worker are you? How can you find out where the Lord may be leading you? This chapter tries to answer that question.

Finding a vision is not the same as receiving guidance

We are assuming here that your vision relates to the longer term; guidance relates to the shorter term. There are many books which will show you how to seek guidance through the Scriptures, through prayer, and advice. To build a personal vision you will use similar principles, but go beyond immediate decisions to your ultimate goals.

Finding a vision can be deeply challenging

Jesus bids us to have faith so that when we say to a mountain, 'Move hence to yonder place', it will move. 'Nothing', He said, 'will be impossible to you' (Matthew 7:20, RSV). Jim Elliot, when he was twenty-one, wrote, 'As your life is in His hands, so are the days of your life. But don't let the sands of time get into the eye of your vision to reach those who sit in darkness. They simply must hear. Wives, households, practices, and education must learn to be disciplined by this rule: Let the dead attend to the affairs of the already dead; go then and attend to the affairs of the dying'. Jim did just that and went to the Auca Tribe in Ecuador four years later. This was the mountain he prayed would move. It did, but not in the way he anticipated. It began to move when he and his companions were speared to death. This event stirred Christians to pray for the Aucas as never before. The wives of those killed continued in love to witness to the Aucas, and, within ten years, there was a thriving church among the Aucas.

Finding a vision for yourself can help other people

Philip Greenslade in his book *Leadership* (Marshall Pickering, 1984) suggests that a leader with a clear vision gives to his people a true sense of destiny, brings coherence to their energies at work, needs endurance for the task to be done, and provides a community for his people. In other words a leader with a vision helps others to have the same.

You may need to rediscover God's vision for your Church, your organisation or your business. But you cannot begin to change the world until you have a sense of what *your* vision is.

BUILDING YOUR VISION

Through the Scriptures

At the Acts '86 Conference, John Wimber described the vision he had had some months after he had started his Vineyard Church. He was reading Matthew Chapter 9, and the conviction came to him that just as Jesus healed the sick, so should he. His vision did not come from his experience but the Scriptures. 'My job', he said, 'is to perform the deeds, to do the duties, the Lord has given me to do.' Today his Church is widely known for the many who have been physically (and spiritually) healed through his ministry.

What are you doing in relation to the obligations set out in the Scriptures? C. T. Studd's motto was, 'If Jesus Christ be God and died for me, then no sacrifice can be too great for me to make for him'. He came to this from reading the pages of Holy Writ. Any biblical vision will be controlled by two dimensions – the character of the kingdom and the personality of the king.

Vision must begin with the Scriptures. So stop and from your understanding of the Bible, ask yourself these questions writing down your answers here:

1) What in general terms does God want me to do?

_____

_____

2) For how long might He want me to do that?

_____

3) Is the geographical location of where that might be
   fulfilled specific?

_____

Through prayer

James Dobson's great-grandfather asked the Lord to give him
all his family down to the fourth generation. James Dobson,
concerned so much for the Christian family today, is in that
fourth generation, and can testify that all his immediate
relatives are Christian.

Do you pray for your children? Your children's children?
Your children's children's children? Or if you are not married
or have no children, the children of your brother, sister, uncle
or aunt? Let your mind stretch to the future as you pray. What
might God have in store for your family? Do you pray for the
husbands your daughters will marry? Or the wives your sons
will marry? Someone somewhere else is bringing them up
now.

Who will your children meet? Where – at Church, in the
street, at school, at work? Who will influence them? How
might your Christianity help or hinder them? What will your
children read, watch, hear, learn? How will their Christian
consciousness be increased? How might it be deadened? How
do you pray for them? How much do you pray down the
generations and so into the future?

What will be your personal vision? It may well come as you
pray for all those in your current context. Vision is about the
future; so pray into the future for them. And as you pray for
others, pray too for yourself.

Your vision may not come from praying for your family.
Paul Yonggi Cho, pastor of the world's largest church in
Seoul, testifies to praying and fasting many times as he
wrestled to work out his vision. Pastor Peter Douglas in
Bristol said 'I receive my vision through spending time in
prayer and getting this into my spirit.'[1]

Amos was a man of prayer. As he interceded for Northern
Israel he saw in a vision judgment by locusts and then by fire

(7:1–6). The Lord heard his prayer, but then showed him a picture of God with a plumb-line in his hand measuring how far the nation was out of true and no longer upright (7:7–9).[2] He prayed and then came the vision.

Through dreams

We have seen that dreams and visions are not the same, but many thoughts relating to the future can come as we consciously day-dream. One survey showed that 57% of people living in the United States day-dreamed about travelling to different places around the world, and 36% of what their future life would be like.[3] My colleague David Cormack often quotes, 'Do not fear those who dream while they sleep; it is those who dream when they are awake who mean business'. Luis Palau at the Columbian Conference in Latin America in 1987 said, 'Dream great dreams and pray great prayers'. William Carey, the father of modern missions, said: 'Attempt great things for God, expect great things from God'. What developments would you most like to see in the Church between now and the end of the century? Think of three specific items you feel would be the most important for the kingdom of God if they were to occur. Write them down here:

1) _____

2) _____

3) _____

Rosalind Allan dreamt one bleak wet afternoon in February 1981 as she recovered from a hysterectomy, of being in a helicopter watching a van go along the road with the words 'Christian Book Service' on its sides. Then she dreamt she was driving the van with all its boxes inside. Then she saw the boxes open and, inside a house, Christian books displayed and being read. Today the Good News Trust which she and her husband founded, are responsible for nearly thirty such vans providing books, videos, tapes, and strengthening many inter-denominational house fellowships, especially in the rural areas of Britain.[4]

Through information

A young art student was copying one of Turner's pictures in the National Gallery. His eyes were being continually lifted from his canvas to his 'master'. He put nothing down which he had not first seen. As saintly John Henry Jowell writes, 'Wise doing always begins in clear seeing. We should be more efficient in practice if we were more diligently assiduous in vision. Looking is a most needful part of our daily discipline'.

Josiah 'began to seek after God' (2 Chronicles 34:3) and as he saw the holiness of the Lord he saw the uncleanness of the people. 'In the twelfth year he began to purge Judah.' What is it you have seen? 'What I say unto you I say unto all, "Watch!".'

What we see happening in the world around us comes through the information we receive. Papers, magazines, television, the people we talk to, the meetings we attend – they all give us information. How do you use and assess it? How does it affect your actions? A realistic vision must take account of the world and its need as we perceive it. That we all see the world differently doesn't matter, as few visions are identical. What I want to try and accomplish may be very different from you, even though we have the same basic information. We may have identical purposes, but different missions.

However 'facts' and 'information' are different. Information is more than just facts. The facts may be numbers, like those in Chapter 2, but information builds on those facts to give intuition, a mental picture, an assurance, an identity. As John Naisbitt points out, 'Ultimately, vision gets translated into sales . . . and the numbers come after the vision. In the old-style companies, the numbers are the vision'.[5]

Facts make you look at the world the way it is, not the way you wish it to be. Information gives you clues about how you might respond to the facts. Information, or knowing your business, is 'being able to bring to bear on a situation everything you have seen, felt, tasted and experienced'.[6]

The opportunities open to women today are greater than they have ever been. But it was the 1975 Sex Discrimination Act that drew attention to how their role was perceived, their careers often assumed to revolve around having families, and how few opportunities were given to them. That is now radically changed and women 'have the right to choose what they want to do with their lives without the impediment of prejudice barring the path to fulfilment'.[7]

What information do you perceive? The vital importance of perception is brought out in the Constable's question in Arthur Conan Doyle's story *Silver Blaze*, where a dog that usually barks doesn't:

'Is there any point to which you would wish to draw my attention?'
'To the curious incident of the dog in the night-time.'
'The dog did nothing in the night-time.'
'That was the curious incident,' remarked Sherlock Holmes.

Through experience

In Book VII of the *Republic*, Plato refers to prisoners who are chained in a cave where they can only see the shadows of objects cast by a fire burning behind them. Since the prisoners have seen nothing else, they will assume that the shadows are reality.

Our basic reality comes through experience: things done, conversations had, sights, smells and sounds. What does that tell us about the needs of our world? Visions from God rarely move us into an entirely different direction. There is a relationship between the present and our understanding of the past. God builds on and fulfils past revelations and then God moves us to a new level of understanding. Thus it was that the fearful apostles could become daring disciples ready to challenge the Jewish nation and the Roman Empire, and indeed the whole world of their day.[8]

Gordon Cosby is the Founding Pastor of the Church of the Saviour in Washington, DC, which began in 1946. He felt called to preach when he was fifteen years old and went for training at a Southern Baptist Seminary. As a Chaplain in the Second World War he found that his perspectives changed in the intensity of life and suffering under combat conditions. He was able to see the results of what was happening to church people, who were frequently totally unprepared for what they faced. He learned that the inner life is frequently strengthened by suffering, and he wanted to found a community which could understand and build on that. He sensed this would not be a normal Church. It isn't! His radical discipleship and commitment to the poor have become a model for many others.[9] His vision came in part through his experience. So might yours.

Experience is rooted in the past. If you want to think about the future, you will need to draw on your memories, 'functional memories' as Ray Bakke calls them.[10] He explains how he began having monthly celebratory dinners in his church to help people recall the previous thirty days. After a time they were able to recall a year or more, and thus able to respond from these memory reserves to the future. Because they were secure in their identification of the past they were willing to act with compassion, courage and commitment for the future. We need similar memories. What are the key elements in your background that you feel are essential? They may relate to your character, your skills, your jobs. Choose three things about yourself and write them down. Imagine a person who knows you well introducing you (in your absence) to a third person. How would that second person describe the essential you? Write down three key elements:

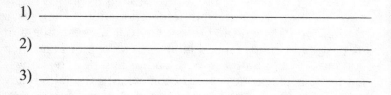

1) _____

2) _____

3) _____

Through your gifts

Why are you here? Does what you do count? Do you make a difference to anybody? Can you become somebody where you are now? Do you want to? Can you 'own' the place where you work? Do you have any rights? Does the work you are currently doing add any richness to your life? Would you show what you are doing to your family, or would you be too ashamed? Is there anyone you can trust? Who can you influence?

These are some of the questions raised by Max De Pree.[11] All are important but are very difficult to answer. How can we find out what our primary gifts are?

Our gifts and skills are helpful in determining what our individual vision should be. Peter Wagner, in *Your Spiritual Gifts can help your Church Grow*,[12] helpfully gives a list of some twenty-seven gifts that he finds listed in the Scriptures. This list is reproduced below. Go through it and indicate those gifts which you believe the Lord may have given you. Knowing what we believe are the things that God has given us is a critical indication of the strength and outworking of our vision, for invariably the vision that we will have has to depend on those gifts. This is the prime reason for trying to discover our spiritual gift or gifts. Knowing our gifts helps the Church as a whole, and helps us to glorify God. The precise definition of these gifts, and the reasons for this particular list of just twenty-seven, are given in Peter Wagner's book. He also shows how to find your gifts if you are unsure. But for the moment go through the list on the next page and put a tick in one box in each row alongside each named gift.

Fig 7: Table of gifts

Gift	Am sure I have it, and have practised it	Think I have it, but have not yet practised it	Do not think I have it but am not sure	Am sure I do not have it	Am not sure whether I have it or not
1. Prophecy					
2. Service					
3. Teaching					
4. Exhortation					
5. Giving					
6. Leadership					
7. Mercy					
8. Wisdom					
9. Knowledge					
10. Faith					
11. Healing					
12. Miracle worker					
13. Discerning of spirits					
14. Speaking in tongues					
15. Interpretation of tongues					
16. Apostle					
17. Helping others					
18. Administration					
19. Evangelist					
20. Pastor					
21. Celibacy					
22. Voluntary poverty					
23. Martyrdom					
24. Hospitality					
25. Missionary					
26. Intercession					
27. Exorcism					

Through your skills

The gifts themselves, while essential, are only part of the scheme whereby we may know what it is that God would have us do. The skills that we have developed are also essential in that determining process. How can we ascertain what are our individual skills? Bernard Haldane in *How to make a habit of Success*[13] helpfully suggests a priority setting process whereby individuals can find out those things he or she is good at. He suggests the following procedure:

1) Divide up your life into approximate five-year intervals, (ignoring the first five years) until you reach your present age. In each of those periods write down one thing you did where, now looking back, you are proud to have been involved. You may not have been successful, but you were glad you at least tried to do it. As a fifteen-year old, a German colleague described spending hours producing a beautiful piece of inlaid wood in an intricate design. A friend described being involved in Church Youth Work and planning a special rally one Saturday so that the church might be at least half full. In spite of much visiting and prayer the dream of a church half full was never realised. It doesn't matter what kind of item you cite, so long as on looking back, you are now pleased to have been involved. There is no particular magic in the five-year groups; if you want to have two things between when you were aged between 10 and 20 and perhaps three things when you were aged between 20 and 30, that's fine, but what is important is that you do choose things which cover the entire span of your life, however insignificant and small those things may now seem to be.

2) Number those individual items and in the grid on the following pages tick which of the characteristics suggested were relevant for the accomplishment of those particular things you did. Do that for all the different items.

3) Now count the number of ticks that you have allocated overall in each row. Which characteristics have the

Fig 8: Table of skills

	1	2	3	4	5	6	7	8	9	10
1. Analysis										
2. Artistic ability										
3. Budget formation										
4. Control (people or things)										
5. Co-ordination										
6. Creativity										
7. Design ability										
8. Detailed work										
9. Economy										
10. Energy or drive										
11. Follow-through										
12. Foresight										
13. Human relations										
14. Ideas										
15. Imagination										
16. Individualist										
17. Initiative										
18. Inventiveness										
19. Leadership										
20. Liaison										
21. Managing										
22. Mechanical										
23. Memorisation										
24. Negotiation										
25. Numerical ability										

	1	2	3	4	5	6	7	8	9	10
26. Observation										
27. Organising										
28. Outdoors/travel										
29. Ownership of things or programmes										
30. People/personnel										
31. Perceptiveness										
32. Persevering										
33. Persuasiveness										
34. Planning										
35. Policy-making										
36. Practical ability										
37. Problem solving										
38. Production										
39. Programming										
40. Promotion										
41. Research										
42. Selling										
43. Service given										
44. Showmanship										
45. Speaking										
46. Systems/procedures										
47. Training										
48. Trouble-shooting										
49. Words										
50. Writing										

highest number of ticks? These show your key skills. Since your vision will dominate your life it needs to be based on achievements of which you are proud. These may indicate the kind of vision that you need to have for the future.

We have now looked at seven areas relevant to building your vision:

1) Through Scripture and its imperatives
2) Through prayer
3) Through dreams
4) Through facts and trends
5) Through the key elements of your experience
6) Through your spiritual gift or gifts
7) Through your skills

All these enable you to begin the essential task of discovering your vision. Pray for the wisdom of God, and that the power of God may be upon you. The Holy Spirit is promised to all who believe. These can enable you to perceive what God may have you do.

IDENTIFYING THE VISION

The letters VIP were given a new meaning in the October 1988 issue of *Decision* magazine. Billy Graham suggested they might stand for Vision-Integrity-Presence. 'Having vision,' he said, 'is the quality of seeing what can be done, what ought to be done, and how to get it done.'

Wait for it

It was a normal day in the Laban household. Everyone went about their business as usual. The meals were prepared and eaten, the jobs started and completed. Time to get more water, so Rebekah took the jar and balanced it on her shoulder. A stranger was at the well. Rebekah was a kind girl and naturally offered to help. Yes, she was willing to give the camels water also. One can imagine her surprise on being given two large heavy gold bracelets and a ring. Even then she did not know that the history of Israel depended on this mundane event. But when asked if she would leave with Abraham's servant the following day she agreed, and history was in the making. One reaction to a stranger and the vision for her life was altered beyond her wildest imagination.

Mary was an ordinary girl, looking forward to the day she would be married. She had weighed her fiancé up and decided that it would be a hard but enjoyable life. He was thoughtful, kind, and unwilling to act precipitately, traits she treasured. When Gabriel came she was asked if she would exchange a normal life for one of embarrassment, uncertainty, and wonder. Of course she was terrified. Her immediate reaction was to seek basic factual information – she wasn't yet married, so how could she give birth? She was assured that God does the impossible and humbly accepted the change. Many dreams were to follow to give practical guidance on exactly what they should do.

On August 14th, 1980, the workers on the early shift at the Lenin shipyard at Gdansk failed to start work. They were supporting Anna Walentinowicz, a crane driver who had been sacked because of her opposition to the management. A spontaneous march became an open-air meeting, where the manager stood on a bulldozer, winning some of the argument. The friends of an unemployed electrician helped him jump on to the bulldozer and said to the manager, 'Remember me, Lech Wałesa? I worked here for ten years, but you sacked me four years ago!' Seizing his chance, he addressed the astonished crowd and called for an immediate strike of occupation. Who could have foreseen the birth of Solidarity? Who could have guessed, at the time, the prison, the political influence, the many negotiations, the meetings with the Pope, Margaret Thatcher and many others that were in store for that electrician? That day a vision was born in Poland.

When will your vision come? No one can say. But some time the telephone will ring, or the messenger will call, or the letter will arrive, maybe the angel will visit, or the Lord's light come through your reading or prayer, but you will know. Habakkuk prophesied, ascertained the facts, sought for information. Why was God allowing the heathen to do such preposterous things? But the word that came was clear, 'the vision awaits its time . . . If it seem slow, wait for it; it will surely come, it will not delay' (Habakkuk 2:3, RSV). The principle is reliable. God's clocks keep perfect time. Samuel had anointed David King of Israel, but even after Saul was killed finally he had to be King of Judah only for seven and a half years. But eventually Samuel's vision of David's kingship was fulfilled. Likewise you too must have patience. Your vision? 'Wait for it.'

What do you want to become?

You are what you have been becoming. Your past with all its heredity and development has helped to fashion you as you are now. But the question to be answered is not 'What are you?' but rather 'What are you becoming?' or 'What will you have become in ten years' time?' If you keep going as you are now what will be the result? A natural extension of foundations already laid or a radical change?

Fancy Jesus calling a despised publican like Matthew to become one of his disciples! But He had the vision of what Matthew could become. Committing yourself to the future is the most important thing you can do. As Tony Campolo puts it in a sermon title 'It's Friday, but Sunday's coming' referring to the death and resurrection of Jesus. The essential you is determined by your parents, attitudes, attributes, experience or power, but who and what you will be is determined by Jesus Christ as we yield ourselves to Him. And He promises to do more than we can ever ask or think.

So be conscious of the Proverb, 'Trust in the Lord with all your heart, and do not rely on your own insight. In all your ways acknowledge him, and he will make straight your paths' (3:5, 6, RSV). Now attempt to answer the question, 'What are you becoming?' Please pause a moment as you read this and reach again for your biro or pencil. What is the date today? Day, month and year. Please add five to the year and write down on the line below the date five years from today:

_____

Now on the next lines write down at least one thing you would like to have accomplished, or one development you personally would like to have taken place by that date:

_____

_____

If five years is too short a timescale, try answering instead, 'What will I have become by the time I retire?' Or 'What will people remember me for?' Some people in poor health may make detailed preparations for their funeral service. The evangelist David Watson, dying of cancer, wrote to many of his friends asking their forgiveness for times he felt he had not been courteous and loving towards them. Imagine you are having one of those 'out-of-body' experiences and are gazing not at your death bed but at your grave after the funeral has taken place. What epitaph would you see carved on your tombstone? If it helps, on the drawing below on the first line write your name.

Now on the next lines write your epitaph. Long-term planning necessitates knowing what you want to accomplish. This is the heart of vision building. Do not imagine it comes easily or quickly. Wrestle with it, pray over it, beseech the Lord to guide you in sufficient self-knowledge to know what you might accomplish for Him.

David Livingstone's astonishing travels came in part from

his continuing stamina to keep on going. He refused to give up either his journeys or his opportunities to witness to His Lord. No wonder that *The Times* obituary in May 1873, commented, 'This is no crumbling marble, this is living stone'. What will your obituary say about you?

Be crisp

Having established the concept(s) to which you would like to work, the next is to try and reduce that to a few short words. A crisp statement, like that of the Los Angeles Headmistress who runs herself and her entire school around the statement, 'I will respect myself and others', which is used as the final arbiter in all relationships.

James Dobson undertakes much marriage counselling in the United States, and his books, films, magazines, TV programmes and teaching have helped many. His father, a Christian businessman, was very special to him. He was a person who spent much time interceding with God. So much so that in his will he asked that on his tombstone two words only be put after his name – 'He prayed'. There are thousands of verbs in the English language. If you had to choose just one to be remembered by, what would it be? He loved? She gave? She served? He helped? He counted? She pioneered? He preached? What's the essential item you feel is crucial to you? Write it here:

He/She _____

Why is this kind of thinking important? There can be a kind of wish-fulfilment in the process, which is why it is critical to search the Scriptures, pray to the Lord, and seek other people's advice. In his book *The Intuitive Manager*, Roy Rowan says 'that this type of thinking forward is used by Stamford neurophysiologist Karl Pribram to describe "those images of achievement that spin us on to creative action". A mental image of some future event can trigger connections in the nervous system that resemble actual experience. Research suggests that the body cannot distinguish between imagined and actual events.' Rowan says, 'That's why a vivid mental picture of ultimate success helps steer an individual intuitively to a desired objective. The reverse is probably also true. A vivid mental picture of disaster steers the individual toward disaster'.[14]

We do need this kind of stimulation. Where are the men and women of vision today? Where are the equivalent of people like William Leech who said he wanted to do three things in his life – be a successful businessman, own a Rolls Royce, and give large amounts of money to charity? God has used him to fulfil all three, and he has donated millions and millions to major Christian causes. The *Manchester Guardian* on July 3rd, 1938, urged the Prime Minister, Neville Chamberlain, to use Winston Churchill's gifts 'in any capacity', putting patriotism above personal rancour, because England needed 'Ministers of vision'.[15] The psychologist Levinson found that men who, for some reason, did not formulate a 'dream' tended to drift from job to job and dealt relatively superficially with their sense of self-worth. Many 'dreamless' people exist, sometimes because their parents belittled them or wouldn't let them go as they grew up.

Vision is empowering. The cardiologist George Sheehan writes, 'Where have all the heroes gone? They've gone with the simplicities and the pieties and the easy answers of another era. Our lack of heroes is an indication of the maturity of our age. A realisation that every man has come into his own and has the capability of making a success out of his life. But also that this success rests with having the courage and endurance, and, above all, the will, to become the person you are, however peculiar that may be'.[16] Or take the Longfellow verse 'Lives of great men all remind us we can make our lives sublime. And, departing, leave behind us footprints on the sands of time'.

Such sentiments can be appealing, but they can be dangerous for Christians. The Psalmist reminds us, 'Not unto us, O Lord, not unto us, but unto Thy name give glory' (115:1, AV), and we must constantly remember that the purpose of a vision for a Christian is not self-aggrandisement, or boasting, but the glory of God. Visions can tyrannise and push individuals to an extraordinary level of achievement;

they can also cause other rightful priorities like family and health to be put aside.

Even so we still need men and women of vision! Who can say it crisply and powerfully, and who can stand behind the proverb 'He who plants a walnut tree expects not to eat of the fruit'. Let us remember, however, Churchill's timely warning, 'It is a mistake to look too far ahead. Only one link of the chain of destiny can be handled at a time'. That is true, so in identifying one's vision what further step is necessary?

We must have faith

In his book, *The Church on the Hill*, Michael Bunker[17] writes:

> My wife Mary often reminds me of that touch of Walter Mitty in me. I am sure she is right, and my sons will confirm it. However, my dreams for the church here are not of that order at all. I have always felt deeply that God wanted great things for St James's. Regularly sharing this vision for the church has contributed to its vitality. Each year, different aspects of our life have come to the forefront of our attention. While most of us greatly value the life we enjoy here now, it is the future that occupies most of our attention, for without that forward look we would stagnate.
>
> I am not the only dreamer of dreams in Muswell Hill. Many of our members share my passion for the church. It is not unusual for one of them to come and see me and share a vision for their particular area of concern.

In his introduction to *Hope for the Church of England*, Gavin Reid[18] says, 'Hope rests with the parish churches and I've seen enough of them to be optimistic. It is true that many of our parishes show little evidence of new life or growth, but an ever-increasing number have exciting stories to tell and can see where they are going.'

Strategy depends on a belief in what one writer has called 'informed opportunism'. We need to face the future with a general sense of direction, a willingness to learn, a desire to listen, and a high degree of flexibility. Colin Benton, now the leader of the New Life Christian Fellowship in Winchester, says it was just an impromptu conversation at a meal queue, and a request to pray for Winchester that started him on the path of leaving a large church and involving himself in a pioneer situation.[19]

The God who has the whole world in His hands has our world in His hands too. He is the prime Guide and Mover. As the nearly illiterate Glaswegian Jew, Scottie Wilson, who was rather fond of the bottle, once said, 'Life! – it's all writ out for you – the moves you make . . .' – he was forty years old before he discovered he was an artist with a talent that few understood – but whose works were avidly collected by Picasso![20]

'Poland has always been a country with faith in the impossible', wrote the Nobel Prize-winning Polish poet Czeslaw Milosz.[21] Poland is not alone. Some years ago Jean Darnall had a vision of lights beginning to burn brightly all over Britain as the Spirit of God stirred people to rise like a mighty army.[22] Derek Tidball's vision for the churches of Plymouth is for those 'not satisfied with entertaining (themselves) but having an understanding of the seriousness of the battle situation in which we find ourselves for the King'.[23]

PURSUING THE VISION

Had God forgotten Joseph? Everything about him showed he was a true and outstanding individual, favourite son of an adoring father. Strong and capable but yet so envied by his brothers that they wanted to kill him.[24] It was many years later after much harsh experience that he was finally vindicated and could say to his brothers, 'You meant evil against me, but God meant it for good' (Genesis 50:20, RSV). In pursuing our vision, what are the key items to look for?

Discontinuity

Not every vision is a smooth continuation or extrapolation from the present. Sometimes the Lord repeats the Abramic call to go and leave Ur. Not for Abram was the worship of

God in his native land, but a dramatic change which was to affect the destiny of millions over the next centuries. 'Go from your country and your kindred and your father's house to the land that I will show you.'

Maybe God is wanting you not just to change the slope of the graph but to move to a totally new direction: one man edited a Brethren magazine for nine years in Bath, but God called him into the ordained Anglican ministry in London's inner city; one Society had been doing vital missionary work in one part of the world for twenty years when it was suddenly asked by a secular government thousands of miles away to start work in their country. Perhaps local external circumstances may bring to an end the work for which your church or organisation was called into being, like the experience of the China Inland Mission (CIM) after eighty-five years in China. But God had planned a resurrection into new fields which has led the old CIM, now the Overseas Missionary Fellowship, into totally new areas.

If you face a very radical change, what questions do you ask? Here are some – answer 'Yes' or 'No' to each:

	Yes	No
1) Is your new work true to your essential, basic, prime calling?	☐	☐
2) Will your new work cause the demise of the old? If so, can you and others involved with you accept that?	☐	☐
3) Are the financial implications of your new task within the foreseeable resources of your present work? Might the risks of the new cause a premature collapse of the whole?	☐	☐
4) Will your friends/congregation/peers be able to understand your new direction and see it as a logical outworking of your central purpose?	☐	☐
5) Will the image given by the new work be consistent with your current image?	☐	☐
6) Can you point to confirmation of God's leading by external circumstances?	☐	☐
7) Do you have the faith to believe that with God this thing is possible? And are you willing to affirm that publicly?	☐	☐

You do not need to answer 'yes' to all these questions. Sometimes when a Saul has to be changed into a Paul, the vision given is sure and certain, and one risks all in the process. But most changes are perhaps less dramatic!

Do you face a discontinuity? How many questions have you answered 'yes'? Are you still going to go forward?

Distractions

Some Christians see set-backs as a 'sign' from God to forgo their vision. That is not always the case. Beware of simplistic distractions from the work you feel called to do. God will open the necessary doors if we are in the middle of His work. Where could Paul go next? He did not know, but that night a vision appeared to him of the Macedonian man beseeching him to 'Come over and help us'.

Walled cities, giants, orchestrated opposition, the Red Sea, resource shortages, new laws, earthquakes, fire, plague, rebellion – all these lay between Egypt and the Promised Land. Had the people of Israel known of these, they might have stayed building pyramids. It took forty years to teach a new generation that the God who had delivered them and fed them and clothed them could and would keep His promises.

The key here is *learning*. As you go forward towards your vision, the most important contribution you can make is to help your church or organisation learn. Progress and achievement and success are important, but the essential contribution is to help everyone in learning. Which of these could apply to your church/organisation?

		Yes	No
1)	Reminding those involved of their history	☐	☐
2)	Reflecting on your experience	☐	☐
3)	Providing models and concepts to aid understanding	☐	☐
4)	Encouraging people to experiment with new ideas	☐	☐
5)	Giving people opportunity to put their learning into practice	☐	☐

Any church leader, church or organisation willing to learn can deal with the unexpected. Training is crucial. If there has been a lot of change in the recent past, then a new vision can be strongly resisted. The call will be for consolidation, to wait a while. In this sense there is never a 'right' time to change – there will always be risk, but there is a best time. 'There is a tide in the affairs of man, which, taken at its flood leads to success.' Knowing the time is a crucial skill.

The *cost* must be measured. The price of the vision will need to be paid. Abram had to be willing to live in a tent even in the Promised Land. He had left the comfort of a two-storeyed centrally heated house; instead of being surrounded by his friends he was essentially alone. Visionaries are often lonely people. Never underestimate the length of the solitary road. Your friends may desert you, misunderstand you, or, worse of all, denounce you. But even the Master trod that path; shall His servants have it easier? Do not assume that your family will always understand. But as the vision becomes clearer you will become more and more unhappy and dissatis-fied with partial fulfilments or the attempts of men to provide substitutes.

The *vision itself* can be a snare. You have had one – can I please have another? Alexander Fleming discovered peni-cillin by complete accident; might he have wanted a further discovery? The inventor of the clever 'cat's eye' road mark-ings only stumbled on his finding when one night he shone his torch at a cat whose eyes reflected back at him. Did he then go and try and discover 'dog's eyes' too? Be content with that portion of the will, work and word of God that you know and understand. One vision every five years may be fine; one every five days is disastrous!

Donald McGavran spent seventeen years as a missionary in India. He worked in small, rural villages with many illiterate people. He was a qualified success as an evangelist, seeing the church grow in his area, but nothing like as much as he hoped. It was there that his vision for church growth developed. He challenged whether schools and hospitals which his mission was running hadn't distracted them from primary evangelism. In 1951 he wrote a book *The Bridges of God* which set out his thesis for church growth. It was years before he found anyone to agree with him. But today there are numerous national Church Growth Associations, a European Association, and a whole Faculty devoted to the subject at Fuller Theological Seminary. He was not distracted from his vision, don't let yourself be either!

Determination

Ultimately a vision has to be *followed through*. Benjamin Disraeli once said, 'The secret of success is constancy of purpose'. This requires both commitment and planning. 'It is commitment, not authority that produces results,' says Bill Gore. Mrs Steve Shirley, the founder of F1 Group PLC, explains, 'If you are not committed, you are just taking up space'.[25]

Billy Graham visited his old college in 1965. 'I owe my vision, my knowledge of the Word of God, to Trinity College,' he said. He then asked the president, 'Brother Bragg, will you pray with me that I'll never lose what I learned at Trinity College, that I'll never lose my vision and that God will keep me humble?'[26] 'An entrepreneur,' said Sir Peter Parker, former Chairman of British Rail, 'has a drive to succeed and get things done.'

A vision must be *capable of exciting* our imagination. Without that it is doomed to failure. Vision bids us stretch our minds. The greatest of faith, hope and love may be love, but hope is still a member of that vital triumvirate. Where then is your hope? Your vision? The whole creation waits to be 'set free from its bondage to decay and obtain the glorious liberty of the children of God' (Romans 8:21, RSV). The true visionary therefore prays to 'him who by the power at work within us is able to do far more abundantly than all that we ask or think' (Ephesians 3:20, RSV). God plants His vision in a person's head and then moulds that person to fit the vision, even though the moulding process sometimes seems to contradict the promise. The day comes when God moves his prepared person into his prepared place – and the vision becomes reality.[27]

The vision must *encourage the individual*. Recall Handel's triumphant climactic fanfare, in his 'Messiah', 'The trumpet shall sound, and the dead shall be raised incorruptible, and we shall be changed' (1 Corinthians 15:52, AV). This sown seed of wheat will become a glorious harvest: 'Sown in dishonour, it is raised in glory; it is sown in weakness, it is raised in power. It is sown a natural body, it is raised a spiritual body' (1 Corinthians 15:43, 44, AV). 'Cast your bread upon the waters, for after many days you will find it again' (Ecclesiastes 11:1, NIV).

It is the hidden quality of a person not the physical quantity that counts. No wonder C. S. Lewis faltered when he came to describe heaven. The echoing cry in his final Narnia tale was 'Come farther up, farther in'. There is no depth we may not plumb, no height we may not scale, no width we may not outstretch, no length we may not go beyond. 'The term is over, the holidays have begun' (C. S. Lewis).

Visionary leaders 'look not at the things which are seen, but at the things which are not seen: for the things which are seen are temporal; but the things which are not seen are eternal' (2 Corinthians 4:18, AV).

Obedience

Campbell Morgan of Westminster Chapel once said, 'Obedience is the one thing needful for further vision'. What if Abram had preferred to go on sleeping that night four thousand years ago? Or Jacob had decided after all to stay in the promised land? Or Peter had remained in Joppa? Or Paul in Asia Minor? But 'what ifs' should never be part of the Christian life. We are called to follow Jesus. Edward England, Manager of the Scripture Union Bookshop, has shown the excitement and thrilling adventure that can result! One day going to work in West London he felt life was too ordinary and unimaginative. He sat down and wrote his resignation that morning and found a new avenue of service which has enabled him to aid the Christian Church much more vitally.

What then is your vision? Peter Block suggests it should be

both 'strategic' and 'lofty'. He says if your vision sounds like motherhood and apple pie, and is somewhat embarrassing, you are on the right track.[28] This was exemplified at the funeral of Martin Luther King on April 9th, 1968 when a recording was played of part of a sermon he had preached just two months earlier. 'Yes, if you want to say that I was drum major, say that I was a drum major for justice; say that I was a drum major for peace; I was a drum major for righteousness. And all of the other shallow things will not matter. I won't have any money to leave behind. I won't have the fine and luxurious things of life to leave behind. But I just want to leave a committed life behind. And that's all I want to say . . .

> If I can help somebody as I pass along,
> if I can cheer somebody with a word or song,
> if I can show somebody he's travelling wrong,
> then my living will not be in vain.

> If I can do my duty as a Christian ought,
> if I can bring salvation to a world once wrought,
> if I can spread the message as my master taught,
> then my living will not be in vain.'

5: GETTING A CORPORATE VISION

Lord Cockfield, the former EEC Commissioner, underlined in one lecture 'Of course we have a vision; without a vision you achieve nothing'.[1] We must now look at how your group may get a corporate vision. The group might be a church, a Christian organisation, or even a business. The vision may be for one part of the organisation – a Home Bible Study Group, the youth in your area, or your department at work – it may be for any group committed to each other and jointly responsible for providing your products or services.

PLAN IN ADVANCE

There is no one best way as each group is different. But some ground rules will help. Plan and set aside a whole day to think about vision and nothing else. You are seeking God's guidance so you must have adequate time for discussion and thinking.

Choose a leader for the day. Often this will be the minister, but not necessarily so. Indeed it frequently allows ministers to express their thoughts more easily if they are not responsible for leading the day. MARC Europe has had the privilege of acting as facilitators of such days for many churches and organisations, and we are always challenged by them. An external body or person leading the day means that their relative ignorance of internal politics can often help achieve a firmer consensus for the vision statement.

What follows in this chapter is a whole clutch of well-tried and practical suggestions for running such a Vision Building Workshop to help leaders when no external leader is available and to inform of some of the techniques that might be used. If you are responsible for leading such a workshop try to ensure it is held in a lounge or other place where comfortable seating is available. It often aids relaxation and thought if the day is held at a local conference centre or perhaps another nearby church; being away from your own premises facilitates more objective thinking of your situation. All your key leaders in the church or organisation should be invited – Church councillors, deacons, elders, staff team, directors, department heads for example – up to a maximum of 20 or 25. It is often useful having a flip-chart and overhead projector available to record suggestions so that all can see them. Try to have someone other than those present responsible for providing coffee, tea, lunch, so that none are half concentrating on other matters.

Some of the suggestions make reference to buzz-groups. This simply means dividing up the company into smaller groups of three, four or five people, usually congregating into different corners of the room all talking together! Detailed preparation by the leader is essential but apart from encouraging others to consider prayerfully where they would like their church or organisation to be in the future other preparation by them is probably not necessary.

You may find that such an 'Away Day' proves popular and if you are not in the habit of having such you may wish to consider holding similar events to discuss other matters at regular, say six monthly, intervals. The exercises that follow are roughly in the suggested order but there are too many to do all in one day. A typical MARC Europe Vision Workshop would consist of sessions like:

9.15 Opening Devotions and introduction
9.30 Session 1: The context of vision: Defining a vision
        (Presenting results of Exercises 1, 2)
10.45 Coffee
11.15 Session 2: Exercises 3, 4, 5, 7
12.45 Lunch

1.45 Session 3: Exercises 8, 12 and drawing up vision
         statement
3.00 Tea Break
3.30 Session 4: What comes next – the planning process:
         the role of the leader
4.30 Closing Prayers

The aim of the day is to agree one or several statements expressing what the group would like to achieve, or to have become, in five or ten years' time. The detailed planning involved is also crucial, but do not attempt to do more in the day than to agree the long-term goal(s) for your group. For example, the staff, elders and deacons of a Baptist Church in Surrey met together for a day in November 1988 and agreed the following vision statements:

1) To take all opportunities to show the Gospel in the local community and the world at large.
2) To structure the teaching programme of the church to enable people at different levels of maturity, and of none, to grow spiritually.
3) To encourage freer worship so that numbers attending increase to perhaps 500 on a Sunday with 300 regularly involved in church activities.
4) To restructure the Home Groups into smaller caring groups with trained leaders so as to allow increased shepherding of the flock.
5) To acquire adjacent land for expansion initially for classrooms and later for the sanctuary.
6) To appoint an administrator to improve efficiency and ease the burden on the pastors.

When the leaders of what was then Gairdner Ministries met to agree their aims, they encapsulated their thoughts into two purposes:

1) To pioneer evangelism among the Muslims of Central Asia.
2) To seek to educate the Church in their understanding of Islam.

From these statements they then drew out several visions.

TOOLS FOR FORWARD THINKING

How can you reach such statements for your groups? This chapter looks at several different ways of starting and running the discussion.[2] Don't attempt them all: choose whichever ones you feel are best suited to your group.

1: Surveys – establish the facts

Sometimes the facts are not known. How old are those who come to your church? Support your Society? How long have they been coming? How far do they have to travel? Do they have children – and how old are they? What other interests do they have? Do they feel part of the family? The *Faith in the City* Report suggested that Anglican churches undertake Mission Audits, and other denominations (like the excellent Baptist AIM) have followed suit. Such a study may not be essential to a vision-building day unless the church or organisation has been through a time of heavy turbulence.

If you do undertake a survey remember:

1) To get views from an unbiased sample (handing out forms at the end of the service and asking for them back the following Sunday only generates replies from the 'keenites').
2) To get an adequately sized sample (asking the two church wardens is not sufficient!).
3) To get a good response from those approached (at least 50% but preferably 70% or more).
4) To have the results analysed by a professional, with answers to key questions broken down by control questions like age-group, or sex.
5) To have the implications of the results put in writing, and in a form which can be shared with all concerned, including those who complete the original forms.

ADVANTAGES	DISADVANTAGES
1. Gives a lot of detailed information.	1. Much work (and sometimes money) is involved.
2. Up-to-date.	2. Requires professional handling.
3. Can focus on particular problems.	3. A skilled interpreter of data essential.

2: Trends

You may already have collected valuable information. What numbers do you regularly collect in your church? Numbers of each service? or Easter communicants? or total membership each year? or electoral roll numbers? Plot such information on a graph. Here are the electoral roll figures for Christ Church, Bromley, an Anglican church which like all Anglican churches was required to revise completely its roll every six years after 1972:

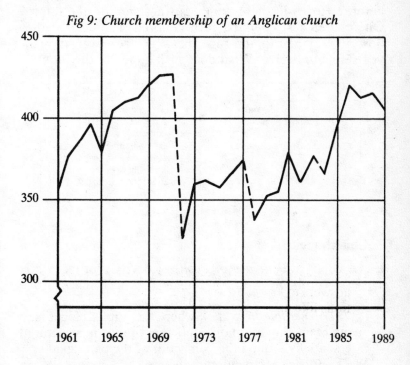

Fig 9: Church membership of an Anglican church

The graph shows that up to 1972 the roll increased on average 2% each year. Between 1972 and 1978 it increased 3% each year. Between 1978 and 1986 it increased 4% each year, and the larger numbers were self-evident but since then it has been declining. What are the implications for the church if the earlier growth should resume?

Almost certainly you will already have useful financial information. Plot this in graphs. What is their trend over the past few years? How does it compare with the cost-of-living index? What is the likely implication for the next five years? Is your financial support reasonably good across most of your congregation/supporters/outlets or are you especially dependent on a few key people?

Age-group is almost always an important factor in churches and Christian organisations. How many at different ages do you have in your Sunday School now, last year and the year before? How will these numbers translate into the future? One church just counting such children realised that they 'lost' 50% of their Juniors (aged between five and eight) in the years nine to twelve. What does such imply for the future?

ADVANTAGES	DISADVANTAGES
1. Data already to hand. 2. Gives an overview of key areas. 3. Often easy to plot ahead.	1. Restricted to data that have actually been collected. 2. Have to assume data collected with the same meaning over the years. 3. Can lead to superficial analysis.

3: Church model

Eddie Gibbs in *Followed or Pushed* (MARC Europe, 1987) suggests (probably with his tongue a little in cheek) five models of churches. These are as follows:

1) *The Venerable Institution* where the primary focus is to maintain the tradition, and the church is structured essentially around the behaviour of the participants.

2) *The Business Organisation* where the key focus is the goals to be reached, and the fellowship is geared around those able to achieve them.

3) *The Happy Family* where the importance of developing supportive relationships is prime, and the structure of the church is effectively a giant informal network.

4) *The Supercharged Community* where the top focus is on the gifts of the Spirit, and the church tends to cluster around enthusiasts who are prepared to be innovative and exercise faith.

5) *The Celebrity Fan Club* where the first emphasis is on visibility and impact, and the church is structured around the influential admirers who can manage and market the talent.

You may smile at these. But give your leaders at the Vision Workshop ten votes each. They can give all ten to one model or can distribute the votes in any way they wish – if all models are felt equally typical then that would be two votes for each one. They are voting on what they consider their church currently *is*. Let them note their votes on a piece of paper.

Quickly count up how many votes have been given for each model by simply asking each to call out his or her score with the leader totalling as he goes along. This is how your leaders feel about your church! Here are the actual results from two churches:

	Baptist	*Anglican*
Happy Family	66	63
Venerable Institution	50	41
Business Organisation	31	54
Supercharged Community	8	13
Celebrity Fan Club	6	21

While the 'Happy Family' model often comes out top, the key differences between these two churches is focused on the second model – a Baptist institution or an Anglican organisation. This exercise can be a useful start to the day.

ADVANTAGES	DISADVANTAGES
1. Quickly and easily carried out. 2. Interesting and stimulating.	1. Can lead to superficial analysis. 2. Final voting can be heavily influenced by one or two people putting all ten points on one model.

4: Stakeholders

Stakeholders are those who have an interest in your church, organisation or group. It may either be a committed or a tentative interest, it may be with or without influence, large or small. Who are the people who in any way at all, are concerned with your group, and who would miss you if you weren't there?

It is worth using a flip-chart to work out collective answers to this question. Ideas may come slowly at first, but after a while it catches on and the suggestions come thick and fast. Thirty or forty stakeholder groups might easily be suggested. Just write them all down – the order doesn't matter. This is a key exercise, one of the essentials, and it should not be hurried. Some stakeholders may be a single individual.

What kind of answers could you expect? Here is a list of forty groups from an Anglican church in the stockbroker belt around London – the list is not given in any particular order:

Local business	Retired folk	Church cleaners
Children	Flower arrangers	Mothers' Union
Local schools	Bereaved	Parochial Church Council
Musicians	The dying	Teenagers
Guides and Scouts	The sick	Widows/divorced
Church's neighbours	Seekers	Historians
Social services	Contractors	Local authority
Other churches	Local paper	Diocese
Medical profession	Funeral undertakers	Handicapped group
Unemployed	Estate Agents	Lonely
Marrieds	Baptised	Grass cutters
Local villagers	Police	Bell ringers
Overseas visitors	Choir	
Parents	Clergy – lay and ordained	

Clearly a huge number of people, to a greater or lesser extent, are involved in that church and the list does not include church-goers and members. Sometimes God is indicated as a stakeholder – of course, include Him too.

Now ask your leaders to identify the five key stakeholders, that is, those most involved with the church who are absolutely crucial to its life and ministry.

Christian organisations likewise can produce a similar list, sometimes rather smaller, and usually more specific but equally valuable.

ADVANTAGES	DISADVANTAGES
1. Makes the span of influence clear. 2. Begins to aid the prioritisation process. 3. Concentrates on people groups not finance or fabric.	1. Almost too many groups to take in! 2. Takes relatively long time to work it through.

5: Stakeholders' expectations

This is a continuation of the previous exercise and will help focus on key issues.

Go back to your list of stakeholders and now ask the question 'What do they expect of the church?' Answers will vary widely. In one church which had no central aisle, the major concern of the 'to-be-marrieds' was just that!

Let all your leaders suggest answers. Sometimes they will want to go back to a stakeholder already mentioned. Try to write down the various expectations as briefly as possible. Here is part of an actual list from one Baptist church:

Sunday School Teachers – Encouragement, Prayer, Recognition, Training
Pastor – Encouragement, Support, Salary
Elders – Efficiency, Commitment
Deacons – Commitment
Members – *Status quo*/Change, Information
Congregation – Lively Services, Truth, Friendship, Enjoyment
Playgroup Mums – Efficiency
Young People – Friendship, Enjoyment, Communication
Home Group Leaders – Encouragement, Leadership, Support
Missionaries – Finance, Prayer, Communication
Residents in Old People's Homes – Visits, Services, Friendship

The answers may not be what you think should be given, but at this stage the focus is rightly on what the leaders of the church at that time collectively feel the various folk involved with the church expect from it.

It is useful then to classify these answers into broad groups. Use a simple scheme such as:

P = Pastoring
F = Finance/Fabric
C = Communication
T = Teaching/Training/Leadership
E = Enjoyment
S = Spiritual Support
O = Office/Operational Procedures

and then write these letters over the appropriate word or the flip-chart list using a different colour pen for each category. Here is the above list marked in this way:

Sunday School Teachers – Encouragement (P), Prayer (S), Recognition (P), Training (T)
Pastor – Encouragement (P), Support (S), Salary (F)
Elders – Efficiency (O), Commitment (S)
Deacons – Commitment (S)
Members – *Status quo*/Change (C), Information (C)
Congregation – Lively Services (T), Truth (T), Friendship (P), Enjoyment (E)
Playgroup Mums – Efficiency (O)
Young People – Friendship (P), Enjoyment (E), Communication (C)
Home Group Leaders – Encouragement (P), Leadership (T), Support (S)
Missionaries – Finance (F), Prayer (S), Communication (C)
Residents in Old People's Homes – Visits (P), Services (T), Friendship (P)

Count up the number of times each letter appears. In the full list for this particular church, P (Pastoring) came top with 27 mentions, followed by T (Teaching/Training/Leadership) 11 times, O (Office/Operations) 11 times, S (Spiritual Support) 10 times, F (Finance) 7 times, C (Communication) 6 times, and E (Enjoyment) 3 times. It is worth comparing the order given by this method with that shown by the Church model: they do not always agree! But this method is based on a more thorough overview over many more of the church's activities, even if the resulting flip-chart/overhead projector slide is almost indecipherable. (It is worth getting someone to type it all out clearly before it gets lost.)

It is then possible to go from this list to a tentative list of visions. For example, it is clear from the above Baptist example that pastoring was a key element to much of their church life. They already had three full-time pastors, but in view of the needs they identified, one of their hopes was to appoint a further pastor. But when the leaders realised that the office/operation element scored second highest with eleven scores, this was translated into the desire to appoint an administrator instead. An analysis of the expectation of their stakeholders led to a specific vision statement.

This kind of analysis is not only possible for churches. Here is part of a similar list from a missionary society. Here the capital letters mean: S – Spiritual walk (for individual); T – Team Ministry; V – Vision; A – Administration; R – Resources; L – Leadership; E – Education.

The Lord – Obedience (S), Commitment (S), Availability (S), Faithfulness (S)

Missionaries – Sense of belonging (T), Sense of joy (S), Prayer (T), Finance (R), Care and Counsel (L), Guidance (L/S), Vision (V), Furlough help (A), Training (E)

Home workers in the office – Pay (R), Encouragement (L), Development (E), Fulfilment (T), Being valued (L)

Prayer Partners – Information (A), Reporting back (A/E), Stimulation (V)

Council – Vision (V), Information (A), Policy follow

through (A), Sense of Involvement (T), 'Success' (T), Sense of the presence of God (V)

Missionaries' Home Churches – Information (A), Involvement (T), Action by Home Society (A), Reporting back (A), Sense of being needed (T), Being part of something larger (V)

Christians and Churches in the field – Advice (L), Counsel (L), Servants (S), Prayers (T), Commitment (S), Understanding (L), Bibles and so on (R)

Co-workers – Encouragement (T), Work support (R), Sense of belonging (L), Fellowship (T), Prayers (T/S), Vision (V)

Missionaries' Relatives – Information (A), Care and Reassurance (L), Involvement (T), Prayer (T)

ADVANTAGES	DISADVANTAGES
1. Looks in depth at wide variety of groups' involvement with others.	1. Is not totally comprehensive and tends to treat each group as equal when some are clearly more important than others.
2. Responsive to changes in key characteristics of expectations.	2. Is based on present activity and does not relate to future changes.
3. Does not require historic data; good for detail.	3. Lengthy to work through.
4. Involves many.	4. Difficult to up-date.
5. Creates interest.	5. Sample bias.

6: Church functions

Why is a church a church? What does it do that other organisations do not? This question has been variously answered. Dr Paul Beasley-Murray in *Turning the Tide* (Bible Society, 1981) classifies the church's work in five areas – *attracting*, *converting*, *nurturing*, *developing*, *serving* which he depicts as forming part of a spring, ever going up and up.

Ed Pentecost in *Issues of Missiology* develops the ministries of the church as *three outward*, *three inward*, revolving around the cross in the symbolic form:

Fig 10: The ministries of a church

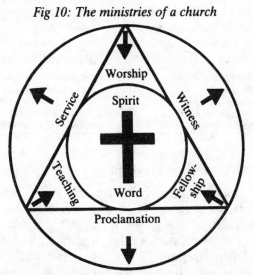

Ray Bakke in *The Urban Christian* (MARC Europe, 1987) suggests six key distinctives of a church:

> Worship
> Fellowship
> Discipleship (or Nurturing)
> Evangelism
> Missionary concern
> Service

In assessing how much your church fits this pattern, take *one* of these sets of descriptions of a church and divide up your leaders into five or six buzz-groups (depending on which model you choose to follow), so that one group would look at 'worship' (following Ray Bakke's model), another 'fellowship' and so on, and ask them to answer the following questions *with respect to that function*:

1) What are the key components in the church at present?
2) How will they have changed, if at all, in five years' time?
3) Why?

Then compare answers and see if any common threads or needs emerge which might help the vision building process. One church which did this found they had almost a complete absence of service to their local community and it was clear that here was a direction which needed to form part of their future focus.

ADVANTAGES	DISADVANTAGES
1. Probes the key activities of a church.	1. Relates to churches and not para-church organisations.
2. May help focus important missing dimensions of church life.	2. It is sometimes conceptually difficult to project these activities into the future.

7: Church/Organisation planning

The second disadvantage given for the above method is a major one. It is very difficult indeed to envisage, for instance, how the worship of your church might be different in five years' time. For this reason, I rarely use the 'church functions' method in Vision Building Workshops, and much prefer the alternative suggested here. It can apply to Christian organisations, as well as churches.

Instead of considering what your church *does*, consider what your church or organisation already *has*: and do this under the following headings, the first four being 'Resources' and the second four 'Responsibilities':

Staff   (full-time, part-time, missionaries and
             volunteers)
Plant   (church, hall, office and machinery)
Finance   (monies received, spent and legacies)
People   (members, attenders, supporters and
             prayer partners)

Community   (area in which church located, or groups
             served by society)
Programmes   (evangelism, training and fund-raising)
Structure   (of leadership within church or
             organisation)
Image   (within the church/organisation, and
             outside of it)

Again divide up your leaders into eight groups so that there are at least two in each group. If you have fewer than sixteen leaders, divide up into four groups and ask each group to take two rather than just one of these areas. Ask them to answer the same three questions:

1) What is this now? (such as, how many staff now? how many people now?)
2) What will this be in five years' time?
3) Why?

Then write down on the flip-chart the answers given by each group to the second (futures) question. Ask for specific answers not general ones. Here are the answers given by one church to where they might be in five years' time:

Staff	– 4 full-time, 2 part-time, 6 missionaries.
Plant	– extension completed.
Finance	– annual income of £200,000; £200,000 borrowed.
People	– up to 235 members. Fewer free during the day and more tired in evenings.
Community	– 10% more homes; centre of town will have moved nearer to the church. Slightly older population because of increasing absence of young households. Local prison completed; pressure on Social Services.
Programmes	– as at present, plus prison visiting and more community involvement.
Structure	– staff-elders-deacons unaltered, but with a link between subgroups and specific leaders.
Image	– members – freer worship; Community – greater visibility; other churches – positive.

Here are the answers, more general this time, given by an Anglican church in the London suburbs:

Staff	– a ministry team of ordained lay and administrative people.

Plant   – an improved hall, so that social
                     objectives and church work can be met.

Finance   – adequate income to support expanding
                     ministry; adequate support for mission;
                     fewer reserves; problems with Anglican
                     quota.

People   – fewer traditional members; more older
                     people; newer people attracted by style
                     of worship and facilities of the church.

Community   – leisure centre; Christian outreach coffee
                     bar in High Street; Christian focal centre
                     for the town.

Programmes   – more care; more prayer; more
                     imaginative use of plant for evangelism;
                     greater commitment to leaders.

Structure   – no radical change, but PCC to represent
                     leadership in the church, and to act as a
                     trustee; an increase in lay team
                     leadership.

Image   – relevant; a focus for the community; car
                     parking problems for local residents.

ADVANTAGES	DISADVANTAGES
1. Can highlight very specific directions for change.	1. Any church or organisation is more than what it currently has; this therefore can overlook tradition and history and past vision.
2. Allows leaders to comment from their area of expertise.	
3. Allows wide ranging discussion with no holds barred!	2. Difficult to apply to a new church or organisation.
4. Does not require historic data.	3. Difficult to up-date.
5. Creates dissonance.	4. Medium-term.

8: Footprinting

This method of vision building is very simple. Take one simple figure relating to your church or organisation – the number of members or supporters, income per year, or similar macro figure. Find out what that number was five years ago, ten years, and perhaps fifteen years ago, as well as knowing what it is now. Draw a large graph on the flip-chart with these values plotted, and then ask for the data for ten years ahead. Now ask each member of your leaders' group to come up, one by one, and mark with a cross what they think the number will be then. The result from one large church looked like this, and is typical of many:

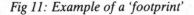

Fig 11: Example of a 'footprint'

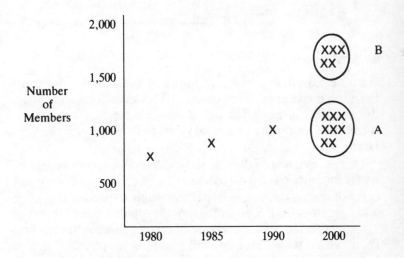

Note that two groups have been formed, shown by the outlines A and B. This is not uncommon. We might call these the optimistic and realistic guesses. The outline looks a little like a footprint, which gives this method its name. Occasionally a third group, lower than the rest, is also found, which might be called pessimistic.

In the example overleaf the greater number favour a figure of about 1,000 members by the year 2000, but a small number (including, importantly, the minister) had suggested the number might be perhaps 1,600 or 1,800, roughly doubling the size of the present membership. This simple exercise can help set the scene for crystallising the essential vision. It is important in doing this that the minister or leader of the group is the *last* to mark his or her position. Don't allow people to fall into the easy trap of following the leader.

ADVANTAGES	DISADVANTAGES
1. Simple and quick. 2. Involves many people. 3. Forces consideration of future on to one key variable. 4. Creates interest. 5. Takes account of experience.	1. Requires some historic data. 2. Sample bias. 3. Inflexible in that it relates to only one criterion. 4. Crude and very subjective.

9: Analogy

Can the experience of your church or organisation be compared to broader types of change? This question can act as a discussion starter, so long as the leader has thought it through. The points of analogy can then be put on the flip-chart.

Our experience of disease shows that once someone has it, it is frequently passed on to someone else. The rate of spread of epidemics is known, and so it is possible to predict the onset and spread of AIDS and other viral type diseases.

Our experience of war is one of retreat and confusion, and then, with a pause for intensive planning, to push out again. Does this kind of analogy help us as we envisage the future of our church? Do we need a period of consolidation first and foremost, with forward thinking coming later?

Our experience of Empire was one of growth and decline. Has our organisation reached its zenith? Has it accomplished largely the task it was given to do? Should it now reduce the scale of its activities and unwind? Should it ever close down?

Or do you hold on to where you are, having lost what has gone, but determined under God to lose no more?

Experience from Gospel campaigns assists organisations to plan effectively for similar events. Thus the experience from Mission England and Mission to London was particularly important in planning for Mission '89, Billy Graham's visit to London in June and July 1989.

Life itself goes through periods of growth and quietness. Where are we in the life cycle of our church? organisation? Are we ready for a period of growth?

The church also has progressed through a number of styles. In the initial Jewish phase it was dominated by the personal approach. In the Greek phase it became philosophical. Under the Romans it was institutional. The European phase made it cultural. The Americans have made it an enterprise. What will the Asians make it?

Such analogies sometimes uncover major parallels and patterns which work in the long term. We may feel that twentieth century social patterns are totally unlike those of say the Roman era, and that Gospel campaigns and military campaigns are too dissimilar for words, but sometimes the thinking implicit in one, is helpful to the other.

ADVANTAGES	DISADVANTAGES
1. Can be thought through by a single individual. 2. Easy to communicate. 3. Long-term.	1. Conceptual approach may be offputting to some people. 2. Biased on experience of individual(s) concerned. 3. Requires historical information. 4. Inflexible. 5. Limited in approach.

10: Indicators

Jesus taught His disciples to pay close attention to the times and seasons and signs. 'Behold, the fig tree and all the trees; as soon as they come out in leaf, you see for yourselves and know that the summer is already near. So, also, when you see these things taking place, you know that the kingdom of God is near' (Luke 21:29, 30, RSV).

As season follows season so there are cause and effect relationships which enable observers to anticipate subsequent events. A rapid and sustained rise in pay settlements usually results in inflation. An increase in housebuilding leads to improvements in the textile industry. Persecution leads to church planting. Ageing supporters lead to a decline in giving, but more legacies. Similar signs are all around for those who can read them.

Demographic changes affect the ebb and flow of church growth. That the UK population is growing older has to affect church membership and attendance. Inner city decline, rural community changes, the movement of the population from one area to another are all relevant, and some of these are mirrored in the stakeholders' expectations examples given previously. Missionary activity tends to reflect the level of witness ten years before in the college and university campus. Ten years after a Billy Graham campaign the number of Christian leaders increases. Major events like a war may cause a whole generation to be missed, though there is an increase in church-going during war.

Economic changes affect church life also. Government indicators regularly reflect the rates of inflation and other key performance indicators in the business, money and public markets. The increasing cost of land is bound to affect decisions on building new churches or redeveloping existing ones. Clergy expectations on salary, housing benefit or car allowances are to some extent determined by the mores of their existing congregations.

The long-term psychological effects of changes in the UK abortion law of 1967 are only now becoming apparent in older women.

Such a use of signs or indicators is often rejected by the church, or neglected by it, though it is interesting that more attention is being given to them by the New Churches, or House Church Movement. Some feel they smack of 'end-of-the-world' predictions, and frequently the statement of Jesus that 'it is not for you to know the times or seasons which the

Father has fixed by his own authority' (Acts 1:7, RSV) is emphasised. If you use them with spiritual discernment and insight 'indicators' of the future can be a useful biblical technique available today.

ADVANTAGES	DISADVANTAGES
1. Useful for short, medium and long-term.	1. Data often difficult to detect/collect.
2. Easily updated once established.	2. May be insensitive to major discontinuities.
3. Excellent for cyclical changes.	3. Needs historic data.
4. Readily identifies turning point.	4. Quantitative data usually needs computer support.

11: Scenario thinking

In industry, strategic planning has developed considerably in recent years. Only twenty years ago, it was impossible to predict the effects of a major economic discontinuity. For instance, in 1967 the Arab–Israeli war highlighted the vulnerability of the free world's major oil sources. Oil suppliers soon used their power and put up the price of oil – it moved 300 times higher in the next few years than it had moved in the previous twenty-five. Countries, industries and companies were taken by surprise and realised that the simpler days of 'trends' and 'cycles' were over and that discontinuities had arrived.

The problem was how to plan for such events. In a film of their organisation made in the 1970s, Shell showed they had three planning departments – one looking to the next ten years, one for ten to thirty years, and one looking at likely developments thirty years ahead. This reflected their concern to plan for unpredictability. In response to the need to think through such uncertainties, 'scenario planning' has come about, essentially based on the thesis that if you cannot predict one future, then predict several futures.

Here is an example of scenario planning taken from an excellent booklet *Advancing into the 90s* by Ernie Addicott of the youth organisation, Crusaders. This extract from his strategic plan shows the technique used for church and social trends.

He took his best prediction of the *Social Scene*, and then drew a worse one and a better one. The three predictions are given below:

Pessimistic Case	Best prediction	Optimistic Case
DISINTEGRATION Confrontation at every level Breakdown of Law Chaos Depression Civil War	FRAGMENTATION 25% children in broken homes 5% teenagers involved in drug abuse Promiscuity High crime rate Hardening social divisions	SOME COHESION 15% children in broken homes 2% teenagers involved in drug abuse Some revival of moral standards Crime still serious

Likewise he did the same for the *Protestant Church* situation, which is given below:

Pessimistic Case	Best prediction	Optimistic Case
DECLINE 5% membership 3% attendance Giving halved Decline in attitudes and spiritual life	STABILITY 7% membership 7% attendance Giving steady Imbalance in favour of SE England Attitudes more positive Spiritual life deeper	REVIVAL 10% membership 15% attendance Giving doubled New Evangelistic fervour

It is then possible to combine these into a nine-part scenario set, as follows:

Social ⟍ Church	Pessimistic	Best prediction	Optimistic
Optimistic	DISINTEGRATION REVIVAL	FRAGMENTATION REVIVAL	SOME COHESION REVIVAL
Best prediction	DISINTEGRATION STABILITY	FRAGMENTATION STABILITY	SOME COHESION STABILITY
Pessimistic	DISINTEGRATION DECLINE	FRAGMENTATION DECLINE	SOME COHESION DECLINE

This then allows nine scenarios, and plans can then be drawn up to cope with each should they arise. The process can clearly be monitored and updated as necessary.

How might this work in practice? Suppose you did a Footprint which showed as your best guess that your congregation in five years' time would be say seventy strong with an average age of forty-five (using age rather than years on the lower scale). This might then be interpreted using the above diagram as follows:

SOCIETY

CHURCH	DISINTEGRATION	FRAGMENTATION	SOME COHESION
REVIVAL	100 members Average age 25		150 members Average age 30
STABILITY		*Best guess* 70 members Average age 45	
DECLINE	30 members Average age 30		50 members Average age 50

This process involves detailed, complicated and demanding work. However, it can be simplified. Here for example, is a simple two-way scenario scene for the year 2000 taken from one of the most well-known Catholic orders:

Optimistic	*Realistic*
More Sisters	Same number of Sisters
Younger average age	Older average age
Four to six novices per year	Three novices per year
Each Sister to gain one recruit	Severe enabling problems because of age
Challenge of community	Maybe less work in schools
Fulfilment of lifestyle	Greater use of volunteers
More open community	Greater financial problems
More emphasis on training	More enablers than doers
Better spirituality programme	

ADVANTAGES	DISADVANTAGES
1. Easy to work with.	1. Lengthy procedure.
2. Flexible.	2. Lot of work involved.
3. Readily reflects change.	3. Broad brush, no detail.
4. Long term.	4. Quantitative data needs a computer to handle effectively.
5. Improves awareness of users.	

12: Drawing out a motto

Towards the end of the Workshop, you will need to focus and
crystallise your thoughts. I have found it helpful to divide the
leaders present into buzz-groups again asking them to find a
five- or six-word statement or motto encompassing their
vision. One well-known Christian organisation who did this,
said that in future they wanted to be 'A caring, daring, sharing
fellowship'.

One Baptist church in a London suburb summarised their
vision as:

Praising + Learning + Belonging + Telling = Growth

Pitlochry Baptist Church in Scotland made an acrostic for
their motto:

Fellowship   – its deepening and extension
Action   – in word, witness and work
Involvement   – of the whole family
Transformation – in the community
Holiness   – in our lives to our God

A church in Warley chose:

REACH TEACH BUILD STAND

Here are some examples of 'mottoes' or slogans from Christian organisations which are sometimes highlighted in their literature or notepaper, and two business examples out of hundreds that could be quoted.

Africa Inland Mission: Reaching out to unevangelised areas, helping churches grow.

People International: Bringing the love of Christ to Islam's forgotten millions.

Overseas Missionary Fellowship: Committed to the speediest evangelisation of East Asia's millions.

Christian & Missionary Alliance: Turning relief into belief.

Church Army: Christian Action for a World in Need.

Church Pastoral-Aid Society: Our Country for Christ.

Trans-World Airlines: Flying people not aeroplanes.

Chrysler Motor Corporation: We don't want to be the biggest – just the best.

ADVANTAGES	DISADVANTAGES
1. Easily remembered.	1. Can be facile.
2. Good for communication.	2. Not easily changed.
3. Stimulation for all.	3. Inflexible.
4. Greater interest.	

13: Choosing the key priorities

Another way of drawing the strands together is to ask the leaders of the church/organisation to choose their priorities for the next five years. Here is an initial list made by one large Anglican Church in the southern stockbroker belt.

1) More prayer.
2) Development of individuals/training for specific roles.
3) Challenge individuals to evangelise/develop teams.
4) Redevelop structures for growth.
5) More finance (aim of three-quarters of congregation tithing).
6) Send out more long-term missionaries.
7) Plant at least one new congregation.
8) Establish training for specific groups.
9) Maintain a Home Group attendance commitment of four-fifths the congregation.
10) More people (up to 1,000?).
11) Research training needs and methods.
12) Be more active in the local community.
13) Build new plant.

A formidable list! But where to start? Each of these items may be classified in two ways – value and time. Value means asking what is the level of importance for the item suggested – is it very important or not so important? Time means asking how quickly the item should be done – urgently or not so fast? Classifying the items in this way may be easily achieved by writing each one in what is agreed to be its appropriate box in the following diagram (if there is disagreement, take a simple vote!):

URGENCY

		LOW	HIGH
IMPORTANCE	LOW	Plant new congregation. Research training. Build new plant.	More active in local community.
	HIGH	Individuals evangelise. Team evangelism. More missionaries. Group training. 80% Home Groups.	More prayer. More finance. More people. Develop individuals. Redevelop structures.

It can be seen that this drew attention to five items in the High-High box. All of these were deemed important, and all began to be tackled, which meant redeveloping a whole new complex of leadership structures, which the Vicar assured me several months later 'was working, but taking a lot of work!'

ADVANTAGES	DISADVANTAGES
1. Simplistic approach to focus on key priorities.	1. Sample bias.
2. Does not require historic data.	2. Difficult to up-date.
3. Creates interest.	3. Conceptual to some extent.
4. Involves many people.	4. Not easy to share.

14: Dissatisfaction is the key

Vision can motivate behaviour by highlighting the key areas of dissatisfaction. Change comes through people not liking the present and being willing to act so that the future is different.

In the days of Haggai the people were comfortable in their own homes, but by putting his finger on the areas of discontent – harvest, expectations, finances – the barriers to action were overcome. For the leader who wants a new vision for the people, the actions are:

1) Heighten awareness of the *present situation* and discontent. Talk about them, preach them, write about them. (Haggai 1:6)
2) Point to specific *actions* that can be done now. (Haggai 1:8)
3) *Remind* the people of God's general purposes for his people and his creation. (Haggai 2:9)
4) Remind the people of what *God has done* and can do. (Haggai 2:5, 6)
5) Push the horizons out. Ask a group to think about the *future* and what is happening in the world at large. (Haggai 2:22)
6) Start the organisation *praying* for the future.

One way then of thinking towards the future is to note what is wrong with the present, and to list these.[3] Here are some of the constraints that emerged at one leaders' conference in 1985:

1) Christian complacency.
2) Elderly leadership.
3) Lack of social awareness.
4) False triumphalism.
5) Lack of sense of adventure.
6) Partisan self-interest.
7) Weak emphasis on personal discipleship.

ADVANTAGES	DISADVANTAGES
1. Provides indicators to motivate action. 2. Easily communicated.	1. Relates to present not future. 2. Does not show what the vision might be.

15: Revelations

Many secular organisations have 'mission statements' and visions. What is unique for Christian groups is the spiritual resources available to us. David Cormack summarises these as:[4]

1) The Word of God
2) The Will of God
3) The Wisdom of God
4) The Way of God
5) The Power of God
6) The Presence of the Holy Spirit

Our God makes known the mysteries of His Will through interpretation of His Word and the guidance of The Spirit.

Those who would think about tomorrow must be prepared to meditate upon the Word, for here not only do we have the macro revelations but the micro revelations – the long-term and the short term. Scripture also gives us trends, historical analogies, scenarios and indicators. It is unfortunate that the Church has become so bogged down in today's world – our faith needs to be imbedded in tomorrow. Christians are the folk of the future, at work for God today.

16: A tool for the micro

Much of the above can apply to the vision building process for departments of organisations or parts of a church. A useful set of questions to ask about each group in your church or organisation, which originally appeared in an article by Stephen Gaukroger in *Leadership Today*[5] is repeated here:

1) What was its original purpose?
2) What is its aim now?
3) Is it accomplishing its aim?
4) If not, why not?
5) Could anything else accomplish these aims more effectively?
6) What are your dreams for this group at its best?

MAKING THE VISION WORK

Where do we go from here? You have articulated your vision, be it in a single sentence or a series of perhaps six sentences. You, and your church or organisation leaders, have agreed the key elements.

What happens next? The vision has to motivate people. The vision has to be an expression of the leader's heart. It has to be worked out in detail. We have to anticipate problems. Change can be expected. Communicating the vision well is critical. The strategy behind the vision needs to be articulated.

Evangelism is the motivation

Ultimately the only vision that can grip a church is to aim for growth. It will not be enough to have a new building for a new building's sake, or to increase the fellowship of the church. Evangelism must be the key motivator. That was the dream of Robert Schuller who built the Crystal Cathedral. That is the dream of those at Above Bar Church. That is the dream behind any of the House Churches who are planting new churches in different parts of Britain. Not growth for growth's sake, but expansion because we live in a needy world and there are dying souls who need to be brought in. Church growth therefore is not just an academic subject; it is something which taps the core of our being and the very life of any church fellowship. Of course the vision may need to be wrapped up in the context of a new venture as in this church:

> We committed ourselves to a high mortgage for a beautiful, warm, spacious building in a main thoroughfare. Today every one of our members would confirm it was worth it. Over the last nine years we have gained a hundred families per year.[6]

You can easily imagine the discussions that took place at that church's General Meeting before they finally decided to take on the mortgage for that building. Can we risk so much? Is it right that we should seek to worship in so much comfort? How can we be sure this is God's will? But at the end of the day their purpose was not just to have an accessible attractive building, it was that their church might expand. While the example may be American, the implications of it are universal.

All Christian leaders fired by such vision have to be prepared to confront the excuses 'we don't have the skills to follow this through'; 'it's the wrong time'. Perhaps people are too comfortable where they are, too tired to change, too busy to take on anything else, too wedded to old ways. Attitudes, activities, the environment, culture, even the organisation itself can all curtail vision. How can you solve this problem? Only in two broad ways – the vision itself, and the quality of the person who has it.

The vision of the leader

Eldridge Cleaver, the radical American author, once said, 'You're either part of the problem or part of the solution!' The essential source, under God, of a vision is in the heart of the leader, a person who possesses the mental power to create a vision and a practical ability to bring it about. A vision is compelling. 'The only kind of leadership worth following is based on vision.'[7]

The leader needs to articulate his vision. It may well be that he, with his closest colleagues in the leadership business, may go through a Vision Workshop using some of the exercises given earlier in this chapter. But their purpose is still only to help the leader know his or her vision. When I'm invited to lead one of these workshops and, at the end there is a potential vision statement on the flip-chart, I ask the leader present point-blank, 'Are you happy with this statement or is there anything you want to change?' Sometimes something is changed, sometimes not. But the leader has been asked to affirm the statement as *his or her own*.

The gathering of a church's or organisation's leaders for such a workshop is an informal not a formal occasion. It is an occasion for thinking, not decision-making. This gives the leader freedom to listen and hear what other people are saying. But *ultimately the leader has to decide on the vision*.

That is the first key stage. The second is to get his immediate colleagues to agree with it. If it has been wrought through a Vision Building Workshop or an Away Day together, then of course most will be already familiar with it. But it may be that the senior leadership will wish to refine it further. They certainly need time to assimilate it, time for them to 'own' it. So if it is being presented to them new for the first time, the leader should say that they will only take a decision on it the next time they meet. Allow time for education or 'vision catching'. *The senior leadership must affirm the vision too*.

Test your vision. Check your signals for its relevance to your organisation. Don't follow the pattern of the Methodist Minister in California who decided to build an educational wing to his church, but having started found it difficult to raise the money required. The price of local property was so high. 'Who comes and lives here, then?' asked a visitor. 'Oh, older folk whose families have largely left them and who are retiring soon.' 'And if they do not have young children, who then will use your new centre?' The minister's face, wrote Tom Sine, to whom this was a true experience, 'visibly blanched.' He had not tested his vision, or in scriptural language, 'counted the cost' of proceeding.[8]

Expect discontinuity. If your vision is a true one, it does not follow it will flow smoothly from your past. The widow in Nain could never have expected on the day she buried her only son that he would have a meal with her that evening and that all the people from miles around would be praising God that a prophet had come in their midst. Nor did the disciples ever imagine that night their boat was sinking under the weight of the storm waters that it was possible to stop the fierce wind with the words 'Be Still'. The totally unexpected happens today too!

The third and crucial phase is for *the endorsement of the vision by the whole Church*, Board, Management Committee or whichever group is legally responsible for the management of the church, business or organisation. The vision must be communicated to the entire body, maybe not in every detail, and that body must affirm their willingness to go with it. It is only with the successful completion of this third stage that the vision of the leader becomes the agreed vision of the group, and the leader's task changes from becoming the inspirer to the person dedicated to making it happen.

What if the vision of the individual church minister is at odds with the vision for his church? Or the vision for the individual who is leading a Christian organisation differs from where the organisation really wants to go? If there is such a difference, it probably indicates the person concerned is in the wrong church or is working in the wrong organisation. For while the leader of a church is there, or the head of an organisation is there, essentially the vision for that church or organisation is the vision of the minister or the chief executive. Uncertainty, indifference or hesitation as to whether he or she can really commit themselves will then probably cause the vision to collapse.

Planning the vision

There's a lovely cartoon of Tom Wilson's of a little fellow sitting rather forlornly at one end of a seesaw, with no one else in sight. The little fellow muses, 'There's some things you just can't do by yourself!' Exactly so with visions. One man or one woman may have the vision but its fulfilment requires a church, a company, a battalion, all the work-force, an army, a multitude to make it happen. Don't think yours is any different. If it is worth accomplishing, it has to be accomplished through others.

One way of doing this is to break it down into thrusts (see *What comes after vision?* in Chapter 1). Thrusts are the three, four, five major areas in which the vision will be outworked. Have six thrusts at the most. MARC Europe has four – training, research, publications and communication. AIM International has five – the priority of evangelism, leadership and development, church partnership, the task-accomplished concept, and the repeatability principle.[9]

The thrusts will of course vary according to the vision. Suppose you have five thrusts. Then they may be marked on a diagram like this:

Fig 12: Planning the vision

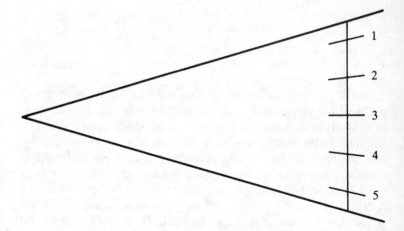

This diagram can help you in the planning process. The vision will not be accomplished this year or next year. But we can start moving towards it this year. Hence reflect the thrusts back to this year, and *make them elements of this year's budget*. They may not fit exactly, but you will be in a position to know what you should be doing more of now and what doing less of in order to fulfil your vision in five years' time.

Fig 13: Planning the vision this year

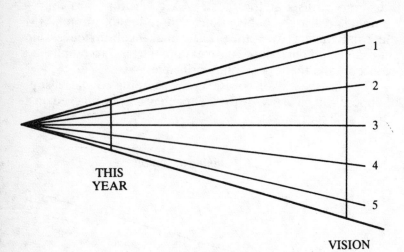

THIS YEAR

1
2
3
4
5

VISION

Working in this way means that your entire programme is focused on your vision. This is helpful to everyone in your organisation or church. The elements which continue from the past know their place in the future scheme of things, the new elements know their relative position also. There is another major value in running your organisation around your key thrusts. Every so often someone is bound to suggest a bright idea. 'Why don't you do so-and-so, Vicar?' Put the 'so-and-so' in the planning diagram. Does it fit within the broad spectrum, like X in the diagram opposite? If so, include it as you are able. If it does not, like Y, exclude it. It is not necessarily because the idea is bad that it is excluded, but simply because it cannot be accommodated within the present vision.

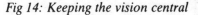

Fig 14: Keeping the vision central

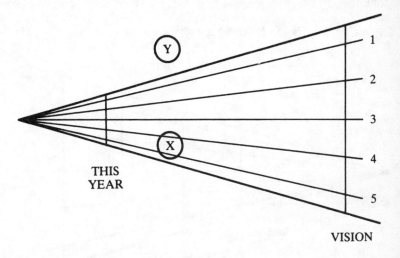

Hence the supremacy of the vision is seen to be paramount, and with that priority clear to all who are in the church or organisation work can proceed.

Developing the thrusts

Once the thrusts are determined, *make one person respon-sible for each thrust.* They will then become the owner of one part of the vision. Ask them how they will work to produce fulfilment in five years' time (or whatever the time period is). What do they hope to achieve by this time next year? In two years' time? Do they need more help? If so, how much? Cost? Manpower? How will they know when they have achieved their plans? Ask them for answers to these questions, which of course you will evaluate carefully. They will then need to plan in detail. How to plan and execute plans is covered in other books, such as David Cormack's *Seconds*

Away! You will then find that the vision is still being targeted, but with key co-workers at the vital points. Once the changeover from what is already happening to the new scheme has been done, you will be in a position to integrate your plans and your controls.

Fig 15: Planning the vision each year

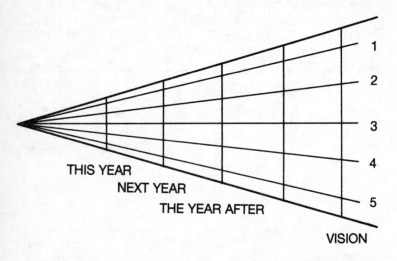

How much will the whole cost? You can never ignore the financial aspect. That's why Jesus emphasised the need to 'sit down and estimate the cost to see if (there is) enough money to complete (the tower)' (Luke 14:28, NIV). Those unable to finish the job because of lack of cash may be laughed at by not thinking it through sufficiently first. But as one does plan the costs carefully, so the vision grows.

What kind of image will people have of your organisation after it has fulfilled your vision? Will its style be any different? Its record? Its public statement? People's understanding of what you're about? Will there be any change at all? Is your vision an integral part of what the organisation is already about or something which will stretch it into areas as yet untouched by it? Will it develop or hinder the organisation?

Will it aid or squash out what you are already doing? Evaluating your future possibilities in the light of the present variables also helps to tune one's vision to reality, and make it in the process a finer and better balanced arrow as a result.

How long will it take?

Every vision has its own time horizon. In this chapter I have often spoken of five years. A vision will seldom be less than three years ahead, but could be for as much as ten years, that is, the vision will normally be *well within the lifetime of the leader*, or the time he or she is expected to stay in that position.

Working out a vision will often take longer than you expect. But thorough preparation is worthwhile in the long-term. The overall development procedure is reflected in the following diagram:

Fig 16: Development of the vision

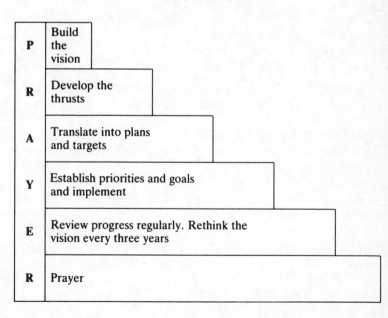

P	Build the vision
R	Develop the thrusts
A	Translate into plans and targets
Y	Establish priorities and goals and implement
E	Review progress regularly. Rethink the vision every three years
R	Prayer

All the time it is important to note the development of relationships, the changing needs of the organisation, the resources available for completion, the overall culture and environment within which you are working, and the image and identity that is being made. Prayer needs to undergird the whole at every stage and in every part.

6: ASSIMILATING THE VISION

'Leadership requires a vision of the future, a strategy to achieve it, and a willing and inspired team.' So believes Raymond Lewis, Chairman and Chief Executive of the Frazer-Nash Group Ltd, talking about leadership to the British Institute of Management.[1] John Naisbitt would agree. 'Once people experience ownership in a vision, the leader's job has only just begun,' he writes. 'His or her challenge is to reinforce, refine and refocus the vision while supporting and inspiring the people aligned with it.'[2]

This chapter deals with post-vision work, describing some of the different areas crucial to successful implementation.

PRAYING FOR THE FUTURE

No Christian vision will come without prayer. The Revd Ian Bunting, formerly vicar of St Mary's and St Cuthbert's, Chester-le-Street, recounted how he and other leaders in his church spent three days fasting and praying. Then came the vision for a £300,000 building as part of the church, and also to act as a centre for the town. It would house such disparate groups as the Aqualung Club, Cruse (for the bereaved), and Boys' Club. The intention was that it would be open seven days a week, staffed by community workers, paid church staff and voluntary workers. It would be participating as a central unit with the church at the heart of it.[3]

Dr Paul Yonggi Cho, pastor of the world's largest church in South Korea, explained how the Lord guided him. The Lord gave him a vision for a church initially for a few thousand people, then 10,000, then 50,000, then 100,000 people.

Initially he did not believe this was possible, but fasted and prayed until he was able to accept it. It was as if he had to 'incubate' (his word) the vision and keep it and grow it until it had matured. Finally the Lord gave him a vision for a church of 500,000 members (though it had reached 625,000 in 1989). 'That's not possible, Lord!' 'Yes it is.' 'But why me, Lord?' 'So that the world can see that even a high school drop-out can build a church by the preaching of the Gospel.' How might we pray for the future?

Geography

God so loved the *world* that He sent His only Son into it. Yet that Son spent virtually the whole of His three-year ministry in a strip of land about 150 miles from north to south, only one five thousandth of the world's land surface. But Jesus still changed the world. A popular church programme in New Zealand in the 1970s was entitled 'Your church may change the world'. The international student prayer diary of the UCCF is called *Reaching the World in Britain*; precisely so, and it is true not only through students.

How can you and your group acquire a perspective on what is happening in other parts of the world? First, you could create opportunites to share what you have seen. What have you learned about the church situation there?

Who goes abroad for their holidays? What do they learn of the Christian situation while they are there? What do they sense are the needs of those lands?

Probably about a third of your congregation takes at least one missionary prayer letter. What is the Christian scene in the area where the missionary is working? Ask them to explain what they know for a few minutes in the Church prayer meeting.

When the news flashes up some happening in Mexico, or Russia or South Africa, do we pray for the Church in those countries? We pray for those who suffer in disasters; let us also pray for the churches across the world.

Which overseas leaders are visiting locally? Can we encourage people to go and hear them?

The clue here is to think broader and wider than the actual physical area of your church. Open the doors of your mind to think and pray in breadth. Take in the existing opportunities and pray for the information people will receive, the impact of those they will meet, the feeling for the area others live in. Help people to pray for the church in those parts, and begin to get a vision for a lost world.

Gifts

When Paul travelled across the then known world he was fulfilling his calling as an apostle to the Gentiles. He had a strategy of starting city churches so that they in turn could evangelise the hinterland. He travelled to Rome, so that refreshed by the Christians there, he could move on to Spain. He was using the gifts God had given him, and urged others to use theirs.

What gifts do your people have? What opportunities do they have to present the gospel in their place of work? How can we help that nurse to live out her Christian experience among the people of her ward? Do we pray for the impact of the words she will say to the sick and her manner in saying them? What of the secretary in that firm? Let us pray that she will have the courage to be honest in the Lord's name, timely in her work, tactful in her talking, so that the image she gives commends the Lord she serves.

What of the professional in the office? How may he or she follow the Lord with pressures of time, perhaps union demands, and the desire for promotion? Let us pray that the Lord will use such people where they are and help those caught up in commerce, government or industry to catch a glimpse of another world.

What are the gifts of the people in your church? Some ministers, like David Reddaway of Crofton Baptist Church, work out in detail the gifts of church members, and then ask the question, 'with these gifts, what does God want to do through this church?'

The clue here is to think of the people the Lord has already given to your church, or your organisation. What might God be calling you to do?

Generations

Hudson Taylor prayed for his children, he prayed for his grandchildren and he prayed for his unseen great-grandchildren. He prayed for the parents of the sons his daughters would marry, for the daughters his sons would marry. He prayed down the time spectrum. The seventh General Director of the society he founded, the China Inland Mission, now the Overseas Missionary Fellowship, was James Taylor III. James Taylor is one of Hudson Taylor's great-grandchildren, prayed for by the founder 120 years ago.

The clue here is praying ahead into the unknown. How much do we pray down the generations and so into the future? Our personal example will help others in our church catch the vision too.

A STRUCTURE FOR VISION

The diagram below shows four key elements in structuring vision. Note the flow to the process.

Fig 17: A structure for vision

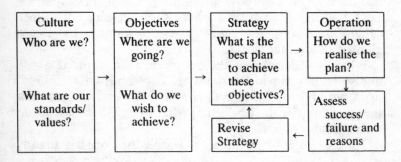

Culture

Our church or organisational culture determines the broad ethos of why you do certain things. Culture is usually summed up as 'the way we do things around here'. Your denomination will influence that. Your leadership team will reflect that. Your history will also be part of that. Through this process you will begin to define standards of what is and is not acceptable. 'This is the way we do things here', someone might say, and it may refer to the style of worship, your methods of organising meetings, communications, or to a hundred and one other items which go to make up what you are. It is sometimes good to try and define what these may be. What are your working principles as an organisation? Write them down. Set them as the key motivators for all that you do.

It is not easy to write down such standards. World Vision held a Directors' Conference in Australia in October 1988, one outcome of which was the affirmation of the following set of standards:

1) We are Christian.
2) We are committed to the poor.
3) We value people.
4) We are stewards.
5) We are partners.
6) We are responsive.

What are the standards or values to which a missionary organisation might work? In the discussions surrounding the formation of a new enterprise, it was felt crucial to identify those concepts which the organisation would be known for. These were:

1) Flexibility in its operations.
2) An active rather than a passive role towards the Christian scene.
3) Accountability at all levels.
4) Indigenous sensitivity.
5) A commitment to personal development among its members.

Such a listing is scriptural in principle. When Nehemiah returned to Jerusalem, and the walls had been rebuilt, he and the leaders made a series of promises (Chapter 10):

1) To keep marriage pure (v 30).
2) Not to purchase goods on the Sabbath (v 31).
3) To service the House of God (v 32).
4) To dedicate the first-born of their sons and cattle (v 36).
5) To give the Levites a tithe of their crops (v 37).

Outside the Edward Ward at Farnborough Hospital is a small notice proclaiming the 'philosophy' of the Ward. Drawn up by Sister L. Portman, it states that it aims:
1) To give a high standard of individualised care.
2) To recognise the anxiety patients and relatives may feel.
3) To give as much information as possible about pre- and post-operative care.
4) To enable all specialists and others to work together as a team.
5) To learn from each other, maintaining an atmosphere which is conducive to this.

Objectives

This is your vision, which needs to include your key thrusts; your aims and how you hope to achieve them.

Strategy

Mr G. J. Pearson in a useful book on strategy[4] suggests that the leader of any company or organisation or group has two key responsibilities – *communication* and *environment*. The leaders *must* take the initiative in telling out the vision. This task cannot be delegated to anyone else. The curate in a church is no substitute for the vicar at this point. The Minister or General Secretary or whoever is in charge should spell out the vision. Even if his forte is in areas other than communication, and though he may have an expert communications person on the staff, nevertheless, the leader needs to articulate before the church or the staff of the organisation the vision that has been given and agreed. By all means let others amplify it and expand it later in detail, but the key responsibility of showing that the senior leadership owns the vision must be taken by the most senior leader.

That leader also has a second major responsibility. To work out the vision, it may be necessary to make structural, person-nel, financial or organisational changes. These, again, are the final responsibility of the most senior leader. That person is in a position to make more resources available to groups at the cutting edge of the vision. Vision can only happen through someone taking the key decisions – to change the budget, alter the teams or amend the physical resources. This is called 'controlling the environment' – that is, amending the external framework of people, money and buildings so that the internal vision can be made to happen.

To match these responsibilities, the leader has two key resources: *knowledge* and *people*. Nothing major should happen in a church or organisation without the senior leader learning about it. The leader also has access to the complete history of the church or organisation and can commission research into programme plans, financial detail, or oper-ational development. Leaders can ask any reasonable ques-tion and expect it to be answered, and frequently can obtain access to confidential information. They have a more com-plete knowledge of the current operation than any other person. That knowledge needs to be used to forward the vision.

Likewise they should have a better overall understanding of the work teams. They may not know each person individu-ally, especially if the church or organisation is large (over 200 strong), but they will have an appreciation of the manpower strength and weaknesses, and of the ebb and flow of recruit-ment, job losses, personnel development, or training. This knowledge of the people enables the senior leader to forge the most appropriate teams to make the vision realisable. No one else can use this key resource: others may have a good knowledge of the various people, but the final disposition must lie with the senior leader.

Operations

These are the detailed plans for the vision. You will need a list of all the component actions, an indication of how long each one will take, when it should be started and completed. Who has the responsibility or oversight for that component? Is that person working alone or in a team? Does that team require any special training, resources, or other help? Who will supervise that component to ensure that it is both completed on time, and to the quality that is required? You may need to draw a critical path diagram to plot these items to ensure your planning is as smooth as possible. Many books are available to help in planning; a popular one from a Christian perspective is *Strategy for Leadership* by Ed Dayton and Ted Engstrom.

Evaluation is a key part of the process. It is rare for everything to go one hundred per cent accurately (and when it does, you may rightly be suspicious). It is always important to learn from mistakes, errors, or time-slippages, or inadequate quality finishes. The review element needs to be built in, safeguarded, and carefully monitored by the leader. Never assume all is well until it is checked out. Build into the programme from the start the times and opportunities to review.

CHANGE AND VISION

Vision inevitably means change: corporate, structural or physical. It may mean new standards, new people, new organisation. It may require new kinds of training, fresh procedures, or a fresh approach.

Some of the consequences of change can be foreseen. Some can't. The essayist and ecologist, Garrett Hardin, suggests the First Law of Ecology: We can never do merely one thing. 'Any human intervention,' he says, 'in the order of things will likely have unforeseen consequences; and that many, perhaps most – perhaps all – will be contrary to our expectations and desires.' He gives as an example the building of the high Aswan Dam in Egypt, which produced electricity and water for year-round irrigation – and which also increased the incidence of disease-bearing parasites, decimated shrimp fisheries in the eastern Mediterranean, and disrupted the five-thousand-year flow of silt nutrients into delta farmland.[5]

What changes, then, must your organisation make to handle your vision? Is a special person needed? A new department? Alternative arrangements? Different procedures? Will you require different systems? Will the existing structures cope? Will new relationships be established, new appointments? What changes can you expect in the people's relationships? Again thinking and praying through the detail often enables the vision to become clearer.

The challenge of change

Historian J. H. Elliott composed an epitaph to describe the decline of Imperial Spain during the seventeenth century:

> Heirs to a society which had over-invested in empire, and surrounded by the increasingly shabby remnants of a dwindling inheritance, they could not bring themselves at the moment of crisis to surrender their memories and alter the antique pattern of their lives. At a time when the face of Europe was altering more rapidly than ever before, the country that had once been its leading power proved to be lacking the essential ingredient for survival – the willingness to change.[6]

Change is not an optional extra. It is necessary for survival. A vision will generate the need for change without necessarily helping it to happen. In a church situation what are likely to be some of the constraints which will challenge you to change?

People change slowly and so do their leaders. In many churches most of the congregation is fairly static, and while, of course, newcomers arrive and others leave, move away or die, the bulk of the people at your church this year are the same people who were there last year.

Tradition inhibits change. It has been said that the seven last words of the church, are, 'We've never done it this way before!' If your traditions prevent you keeping up with the times then you will find eventual change harder and more cataclysmic. You must constantly try to steer between scriptural principles and cultural conservation.

Weariness. Many church people are highly active, and involve themselves in meetings, friendly visits and helping others. Change requires energy, and faced with it many find they no longer have what it takes physically and mentally to behave differently.

Fear of stepping out of line. More perhaps of a snare to the leadership than the average church member or church-goer. You may be unwilling to do something different because no other church in your town is doing anything similar.

Loss of confidence. All of a sudden, in *the* area where you would expect assurance and strength, an uncertainty comes in and knocks your confidence aside. 'I'm not sure,' says the leader in the pulpit.

Complacency. The need for change is lost on some people. They are very happy, as they are, thank you very much. Yours is a nice idea, but not for now. Tomorrow maybe.

Partisan self-interest. It is not too difficult to go one's own way in a church despite the opportunities for collaborators. The Sunday School decides to initiate its own support for a missionary, rather than go through the Missionary Committee for example.

Isolation. Not dissimilar to a lack of confidence, and to a fear of stepping out, some churches are inhibited from changing because their people sense they are different, or lonely, and do not wish to increase their guilt by doing anything which might threaten it.

Instant solution Christianity. People expect a vision today and for the solution to be worked out tomorrow. Planning and careful strategising are not the order of the day here.

Recognising too many constraints. At one conference looking at the problems and opportunities facing the British church today, delegates numbered twice as many problems as opportunities! It is so much easier to say, 'It's too difficult' and so hard to acknowledge, 'Let's try it at least once!'

These difficulties can be consolidated into four main areas – opposition, facing set-backs, losing one's way, and tiredness. How can you cope with them?

Coping with change

In the MARC Europe seminar on the Management of Change, David Cormack sometimes uses a mathematical type expression to talk about change. (He is developing this in a forthcoming book called *Change Directions*.) It looks like this:

$$C = f(D + V + B + F) > £$$

The 'C' stands for *Change*, and the 'f' means that it is a *function* of four things. The first of these, D, is *Dissatisfaction*. At one stage in Egypt the Israelites were quite content. Though a Pharaoh who 'knew not Joseph' had arisen and made them slaves, yet life was not unduly hard. Employment was guaranteed, reasonably normal social life was allowed, food was plentiful, and the people became satisfied with their lot. There was no question of moving them. But then came the order to kill the male babies, and the people began to become discontented. Then, and only then, was Moses sent to call them out of the land. Likewise with us. We may not want to change if things are too comfortable. Once they become uncomfortable, then attitudes often change.

The V stands for *Vision*. There can be little change without some indication of what is going to happen. The Israelites were told of 'a land of milk and honey' (a superb summary statement incidentally) and this became their vision. Moses did not mention the problems of crossing the Red Sea, the barrenness of a desert, the thunderings of Sinai, forty years of wandering, or the fact that only Joshua and Caleb would actually make it.

The B stands for *Belief*. Is there something or someone who can be trusted to see the change through? The stick which became a serpent, the river turning to blood, the frogs, the gnats, the flies, the death of the animals, the boils, the hail, the locusts and the darkness were more than sufficient to make the Israelites trust Moses. Pharaoh's heart might be hardened despite so many miracles, but their impact on the Israelites was to bind them to their leader.

The F stands for *First Step*. It is crucial to spell out the first step that has to be taken. For the Israelites this was the killing of a lamb or young goat, and painting the lintels of their doorway with its blood. How this would get them to the promised land was not stated, but Moses was very certain that this was what they must do. So they did it. As a consequence they found a mightier miracle than they could have dreamed – the Egyptians begging them to go and giving them all their gold and silver to encourage them to get out.

These four elements form change. But change will not take place unless together the benefits can be seen to outweigh the disadvantages or cost (the £ sign). The Israelites saw the weeping Egyptians, mourning the loss of their first-born sons, and decided they did not want to stay. They treasured their families. Too many had already had children drowned, so they took their possessions, their cattle, and the Egyptian jewellery and fled.

Heraclitus (*c* 500 BC) was perhaps in a pessimistic mood when he wrote 'Nothing endures but change'. In a church the pastor is the key player. But leadership comes not only through the pastor but through many other leaders, such as those responsible for Home Bible Study Groups. In a Christian scene we always need to allow for the Holy Spirit. He often can make things happen much more radically and quickly than we can anticipate. The final call for the Israelites was actually quite short notice – just fourteen days (Exodus 12:6), and what God did then, He sometimes does now. We just have to be willing to risk walking with Him.

RISK AND VISION

There is always a risk with vision. When Bracknell Baptist Church stated they needed £2.8 million to build their magnificent new church they felt sure that the money would come in. They had faith. They had prayed. They had seen some confirmations. But it was still a risk. But the Lord honoured that risk, and the necessary finance was found.

The challenge to your vision may be considerable. You may be challenged by the increasing amount of discontent. You may find it difficult to articulate the vision. You may need to spell out the first steps to be taken. You may need to release the power within. Or to plan the whole so that it is manageable – to pace the change in ways in which your people can understand. You may need to avoid major changes in direction. You may need to encourage, to get people involved. But whatever is needed will require some element of risk and of sticking one's neck out.

The price of change is not always or only financial. It can be spiritual, emotional, physical, social. It can involve loss, uncertainty and stress. But underlying that price is the risk that has to be taken.

Risk and faith are linked. The man of faith fearlessly risks the reputation of his Lord and is often vindicated at the time when the darkness seems greatest. Daniel was willing to risk his life because he believed in prayer. David called on the character of God as he ran to fight Goliath who had spurned Him. Peter may have thought twice as he prayed for Dorcas to come back to life. Men and women of God do not find risk-taking easy but do so with an assurance that this is the Will of God.

So it must be with us. Lord Wavell, the penultimate Viceroy of India, wrote in his diaries about the British Cabinet, 'They profess their desire to give India self-government. But they will take no risk to make it possible.' If our vision is strong enough, we must take the risk to make it happen. Occasionally I have met a church where the need for change is evident, where discussions about change have taken place, where the leaders agree verbally that change must happen, but at the crucial point back down and will not take the risk. Nothing is more tragic. As G. K. Chesterton once wrote, 'It isn't that they can't see the solution. It is that they can't see the problem.'

Dr Samuel Zwemer, sometimes called the Apostle to the Muslims, wrote in his *Call to Prayer*: 'The Alpine climber who is trying to reach a summit can, on the upward path, scarcely see his goal except at certain fortunate moments. What he *does* see is the strong path that must be trodden, the rocks and precipices to be avoided, the unbending slopes that become even steeper. He feels the growing weakness, the solitude and the burden. And yet, the inspiration of the climber is the sight of the goal. Because of it, all the hardships of the journey count for naught.'[7] He risked his all for the sake of winning Muslims to Christ.

Graeme Irvine, now President of World Vision International, was Chairman of the group that formulated the proposals in the mid-1970s to create the International Office. It was a radical change for the organisation that then existed. In his summarising paper, he said, 'It takes little faith to take a little risk.' Exactly so! How great is your faith? What risk will you take? Will you go all the way so that your vision may be fulfilled? Lee Iacocca says, 'If you take no risks, you do nothing.'[8]

Risk-taking and security

The ability to take a risk is related to the security of the individual taking that risk. One's level and security may be traced to a kind of Maslow hierarchy, a system so-called after the researcher who identified the basic human needs. The most essential need is to survive – to have enough food and air. Then we require safety and security. Assured of these we look for friendships and relationships, and after these seek value in the eyes of our associates. The highest need is that growth which comes from serving others. How may this system apply to the Church?

The lowest level is simply that of *survival*. We need to have a core of church members, adequate finance, plant and

Fig 18: The Christian Maslow hierarchy

housing and transport for the church leader, and similar features in a church organisation. The things necessary to survive personally (food, shelter, clothing) are reflected in what is the minimum when you talk of 'my church'. Surviving also means continuing membership, a type of status. Thus the leader can give status to others because he can offer membership and the security that brings.

If the church or organisation is to survive it needs to feel *safe* without fear of a merger with another parish, takeover by another group or inadequate cash flow. A warmth level comes from the fellowship. This assumes a model in the leader's mind of what he or she will feel comfortable with. Team members are highly motivated when what they are asked to undertake enables them to be the kind of person they want to be.

Above safety lies *affiliation*, the ability to perform. Your second level leadership support you, your deacons or council affirm you. You seek then to give teaching to deepen that fellowship and to increase the call of discipleship and evangelistic concern. This assumes that belonging to your church means something – members are expected to be involved in some types of activity. Working with your organisation satisfies your employees because it enables them to do what they are wanting to do. With a strong sense of affiliation, you are probably willing to take risks.

Esteem comes above affiliation, and may be reflected from the approval of your Superintendent, Bishop, Trustees, District Commander or Chairman. Here there is an affirmation from the leadership level above you, giving you strength as a consequence. Few of us can exist as isolated individuals. Giving and receiving love is essential. Just as each member of your team wants to be wanted, so naturally you do too. There is a danger here, however, that wanting to be loved can inhibit taking a risk if you fear that the relationship might be weakened as a consequence.

The highest step is *service*. Fulfilment comes from growth. Paul talks of having no more use of childish ways now that he is a man (1 Corinthians 13:11). Little children often describe what they will do 'When I'm bigger'. Growth reaches its peak in adulthood, and the desire for service is also strongest then. It is at this level too that risk-taking can be easier, as you have the security of all the other levels below you. Your desire is to achieve the full potential of your church, your organisation, your specialist ministry.

COMMUNICATING VISION

The actual vision has to be spelt out so that all may see, hear and read. This is one of the key tasks of the senior leaders. How may a vision then be best communicated? Three broad rubrics are suggested below.[9]

Simple words

1) Write the vision initially in one sentence. This is your core vision concept.
2) Use words familiar to your audience.
3) Use clear, unambiguous words.
4) Use active and doing verbs rather than passive ones.
5) Be as short and crisp as possible.
6) State one idea at a time. Do not put two into one sentence.
7) Frame the statement in the positive.

8) State the particular not the general. Beware of abstractions.
9) You are aiming for a response. Therefore be specific.
10) Focus on the future not the past.

As an example of how this may work out in practice, take the vision statement of the Diocese of St Andrew in Scotland, noticing how they have used the initials of their name.

'By 2000, the Episcopal Church in the Diocese of St Andrew will, through the Spirit of Truth, be:

Affirming   God's world.
Nurturing   God's people.
Discovering Christ in others.
Receiving   forgiveness.
Embracing   the disadvantaged.
Witnessing   to God's love.'

The ecumenical, social and evangelistic concerns are readily seen. Their thrusts were to:
1) Support the clergy
2) Create a climate for change
3) Engagement with society.

They wanted to impact their neighbourhood in new ways – 'We are your community church'.

Another Scottish example comes from the Roman Catholic Archdiocese of Glasgow. Posters with a picture of the Archbishop have the clear slogan 'Together for the Nineties', followed by an explanation: 'We are moving in Glasgow towards a church which is – a community of love, of people who care, responding to the needs of men and women today, guided by God's plan for us'. Their thrusts are:
1) To experience renewal.
2) To experience salvation.
3) To establish house communities.
4) To engage in evangelisation.
5) To respect the traditions.

Simple numbers

Use some numbers. 'We have 20 people working on this now.
In 5 years' time we aim to have 100' – such statements capture
the essence of the vision. For emphasis the numbers should be
expressed as figures.

Avoid giving numbers a spurious and confusing degree of
accuracy, by only using numbers to two significant figures.
Not 'We aim to decrease our cost/income ratio from 28.67%
to 19.23%', *but* 'We aim to decrease our cost/income ratio
from 29% to 19%', and, if spoken, it would be better to say
'We aim to decrease our cost/income ratio from the nearly
30% it is at present down to 20%.' This allows readers or
listeners to grasp, and retain the figures more easily.

If you are using numbers of four or more figures, use
commas or spaces to distinguish groups of three figures. So
you would write, 'we need to raise £1,700,000' rather than 'we
need to raise £1700000'. Alternatively, if you are talking in
millions you can keep the two major figures and write as, 'we
need to raise £1.7 million'.

When tabulating figures, order the numbers in the tables in
some constant and logical way, for example by moving from
the greatest to the least in the major column, or alpha-
betically, or geographically in the headings. Identify each
table with an explanatory caption.

When showing numerical comparison, set up the table
vertically, rather than horizontally, especially if the emphasis
is on change over a period of time. The eye can contrast these
more easily.

Not:

	1989	1991	1993	1995	1997
Project income	£110,000	£220,000	£450,000	£870,000	£1,500,000

But:

Year	Project Income
1989	£110,000
1991	£220,000
1993	£450,000
1995	£870,000
1997	£1,500,000

Explain the gist of your table in accompanying text. Thus the table under 'Project Income' might be followed by a statement such as 'We are aiming to double our project income roughly every two years for the next decade'.

Give trend or other comparative data. Whenever possible, and, particularly in longer columns of figures, show a summary measure at either the beginning or the end to provide a point of comparison. Averages are often used in this way, but be careful not to use these too much. As John Naisbitt comments 'we lose all intelligence by averaging'.[10]

Church Expenditure

	Salaries	Stationery	Heating
1989	£10,500	£5,000	£5,000
1990	£11,500	£6,000	£4,600
1991	£13,100	£7,000	£6,000
Average	£11,700	£6,000	£5,200

Underline headings only to show how far the heading applies, for example in the above table 'Church Expenditure' covers all three headings, but not the years in the left hand column. The subheadings on the line below should have equal spaces between the columns of figures (and not necessarily between their headings). Do not abbreviate table headings. Avoid heading a column with a caption like 'thousands' or '£000s' and then printing smaller numbers below as this misleads many ordinary readers, even if it is clear to accountants! Always justify your figures to the right-hand side. If your table includes both numbers and percentages, it is often helpful to print the percentages in italics (a practice followed in the *UK Christian Handbook*). Indicate the units in each column clearly.

Simple visuals

Diagrams allow for the story or picture behind the figures to be clearly seen. The key therefore is simplicity.

A graph, pie chart, bar chart or picture can sometimes save a thousand words. The essence of the table about project

income above can be more forcibly communicated through a
bar chart such as given below. This especially aids those not
familiar with drawing the story from a series of figures. A bar
chart gives a better looking diagram than a simple graph,
although both are telling the same story.

Fig 19: Anticipated income over the next decade

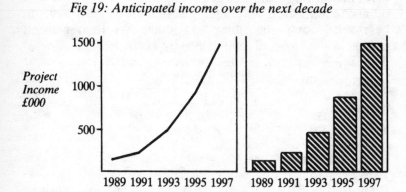

Always give a diagram a title or caption that, as for tables,
clearly indicates the content. Graph axes should be labelled
accurately, and the vertical axis should normally start at zero
without discontinuity to avoid confusion.

Pie charts. Do not usually show sections for data representing
less than 10% of the whole. Show larger sectors in darker or
denser shadings. Similarly, on maps or other diagrams showing numbers in comparison use darker tints for higher numbers so that the shading used by itself gives an indication of
the story depicted.

Pictures/models. You might ask an artist to draw an impression of what the final project will look like. Rather as a new
office block is shown on the advertising in its finished glory.
Not every vision can be pictured, but if yours can be, a picture
will aid the communication process tremendously. Let people
see what the new church or the new extension will look like. If
necessary show them the architect's blueprint, rather than

nothing visual at all. See the examples on the following pages.

Even better than a picture is a model. When Robert Schuller wanted to present his vision of a Crystal Cathedral he had a model made and at the Annual Church Meeting in 1967 dramatically used it to encourage the congregation to support the venture. They did, and raised $17 million in the process to do so.

Dale Carnegie once said, 'The best argument is that which seems merely an explanation.' This is the communication of your vision. Build on the dissatisfaction. Explain the vision or dream not only in terms people will understand, but related to their position. If they find the present building cramped then indicate how the new building will give more room. If they find the present chairs or pews hard, then mention the softer covering the new ones will have.

Help the individual listener to 'own the goal' you are presenting. Therefore give him or her a chance to ask questions, and to comment at an early stage. The fulfilment of a vision is often the individual motivation for many people. Therefore help everyone to see the part they must play.

Anchor the implications of your vision to the present. It is essential to plan and to plan for contingencies. The *Titanic* was planned down to the last detail, but the architect never thought through the problem of meeting an iceberg half a mile away when steaming at twenty knots.

Share your vision by expressing it in different ways. By all means indicate how many people, or how large a building, or the number of books or whatever you will touch or use or distribute. Numbers are an important part of the process. But don't leave it there. Some people find numbers overwhelming. Tell out your vision instead in terms of the skills you will be using. What gifts will you be calling upon in your organisation? People with special – or ordinary! – abilities to do what?

Above all focus on the future and the impact the concluded vision will have. Show how the project you have in mind will help further the Kingdom of God, and bring glory to the name of Christ. Dag Hammarskjöld, the Swedish Statesman and

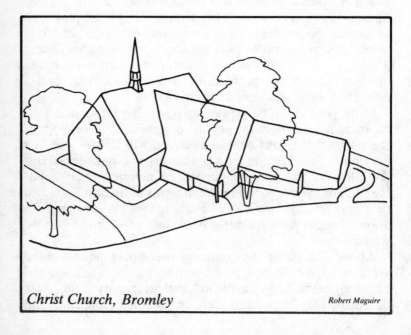

Bracknell Baptist Church

Christ Church, Bromley   *Robert Maguire*

St Chad's Church, Derby

PLAN for the FUTURE

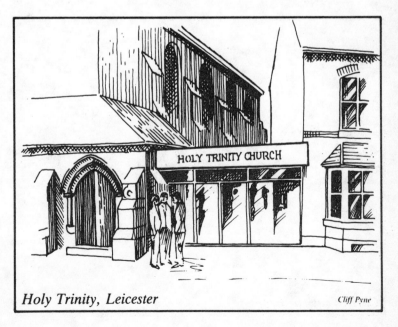

Holy Trinity, Leicester

Cliff Pyne

First Secretary-General of the United Nations wrote, 'Only he who keeps his eye fixed on the far horizon will find his right road.' 'Where there is no vision, the people perish' (Proverbs 29:18, AV).

7: RUNNING WITH THE VISION

It was the largest church I had seen at that time, and was almost certainly the largest in Johannesburg, and maybe the largest in South Africa, and probably all Africa. A beautiful semi-circular building seating 5,000 people, with the most modern lighting and sound reinforcement system it was possible to have. It was 1987 and I had the privilege of a short business visit to South Africa.[1]

It was a pentecostal church, and that morning the pastor of Rhema Church, Revd Ray McCauley was preaching on his vision for the church. A tall, perceptive man with a commanding physical appearance, I discovered, talking to him later, that he had been third in the Mr Universe competition in the mid 1970s. Trained in the United States, he was given a vision by God 'to grow a church for thousands of people'. On his first Sunday back in South Africa in 1982, he asked his parents, then still not Christians, if he could hold a worship service in their house. Somewhat surprised they agreed, and thirteen came. Forty came the following week. By the third week the house was far too small and by the end of the month they had to hire a local hall. After a year they hired the local cinema, and when this thousand-seater building proved again insufficient, moved to a 2,500-seater concert hall. With that filling rapidly the decision was taken to build the present church. It was more than just a church. A school for the children of church members was under construction and a large bookstore had been completed, as had a television studio and separate video cassette shop.

I was impressed with the modern office accommodation used by the pastor and the fifteen senior pastors working with him. In addition there were over a hundred others involved on a full-time or part-time basis. Clearly part of the success of their church was because of its thorough administration and support structures.

Such clear organisation was worked out in detail. To help visitors, every steward or stewardess in the church that Sunday was identified by their distinctive mauve and grey suit or dress. I learned that the same dedication and thoroughness were shown in each of the church organisations. You would like to join the band that plays on Sunday? That means you must attend every practice on a Thursday evening (I think you were allowed to miss one every three months), and must come to the church one hour before each service and spend time in intercession for that service. If these conditions were too onerous, then you would not be accepted.

It was clear that the glory of the church's growth was given to God. Many prophecies of its success had been made. In the entrance to the office suite was a lovely copper relief of a huge eagle with the first words of the prophecy given by Reinhard Bonkke when he had opened the church, 'The eagle has landed' with the thought that the same power would spread throughout the land and indeed the world. The church had a world vision and not purely a South African one. They obviously wished to reach local people, bussed in every Sunday a good number of black people from the townships, and had plans to reach Johannesburg and other parts of their country. But it went further, and they were implementing plans for ensuring that the message of their church went to key people across the world.

What were the key gifts of the leader of such a church? An ability to believe in God even for the seeming impossible, a warm open trust in the working of the Holy Spirit in every person and decision, and the core strength of effective leadership. Ray McCauley may be called pastor, but he is a leader of men and women. In some ways it is perhaps the latter which is the crucial gift. If a summary was made of the major elements involved in fulfilling this vision, the key factors would be:

1) The vision grew out of the leader's heart. It was not just an intellectual idea, it burned within him a deep fiery emotion. He wanted to see 'thousands of people' following Christ.

2) The vision was specifically earthed. The church may have had 5,000 seats now and 10,000 members, but the desire was to see 25,000 members by the end of 1992 (a five-year target) with at least four services every Sunday to accommodate them all.

3) The vision also had short-term (twelve-month) goals. The service I heard spelt out the plans for the current year. These included finishing the ground floor of the school, extending the church's seating arrangement to 6,000 seats, and regularly sending tapes of the church's services to fifteen cities outside South Africa.

4) The vision was well planned. The church's structure revolved around the team meeting that took place every Wednesday, when not only were all the pastors present, but a review was made of particular departments (like the Youth Work, Band, Bookstore) in the church. Each department was required to report every second week and say what had happened since they last reported and what they hoped to do in the next fortnight. Each department had a twelve-month goal and the success of meeting these was monitored. Of particular importance was the statement of future plans – the leadership wanted to make sure that no part of the church was planning anything which would contradict or undermine the overall long-term plans.

5) The vision was regularly assessed. Frequent team meetings took place. The finance was carefully watched every week.

6) The vision was communicated to all. The first Sunday of the year the pastor preached on the long-term vision for the church. Everyone was thus reminded of where they believed and trusted the church was going. During the year the short-term goals were also articulated, as happened the Sunday I was there. Note that it was the

pastor who preached these sermons – this vision building task was not delegated to anyone else. He was the prime owner of the vision and he preached it powerfully and regularly.

7) The vision was backed by excellence in ministry. They strove to make the whole as consistent as they were able. Every part of the church was planned so that 'all things were done decently and in order' (cf 1 Corinthians 14:40). As part of this backing was the supreme recognition that it was God's work and that without this nothing was possible. They therefore 'believed God for everything else' as Pastor McCauley said.

You may protest that your vision is nothing like that. Of course not! The Scriptures show that the same vision or dream very rarely comes to different people – only Daniel with Nebuchadnezzar's statue, and Joseph with Pharaoh's cows and wheat, and in both instances the repetition was for the purpose of explanation. Rarely does the same vision come to the same person twice – Ezekiel seemed to see the living creatures of the God of Israel twice since he comments on it 'their faces had the same appearance as those I had seen' (10:22, NIV).

Your vision is precisely that – *your* vision. It is no one else's. If it is to be fulfilled, it is because you will begin the fulfilment process – because you act on it. The framework of your context must be recognised, the Scriptures must be interpreted, the vision must grow out of your heart. It may need to be passed on to others so that the team is gripped by the vision and hundreds, perhaps thousands will follow it, but the essence of the vision is what *you* believe the Lord wants *you* to do.

John Stott comments that the wise person 'knows that nothing is more important than to discover the general Will of God for all His people in Scripture; and to discover the particular Will of God for each individual, partly from Scripture, partly in prayer, partly through discussing the issue with others, and partly through using the minds God has given us.'

But once you know what God wants you to do – well, don't just stand there, do something! A well-known proverb says,

'A journey of a thousand miles begins with a single step'. Take that step today. And may the blessing of the Lord be upon you.

NOTES

Chapter 1

1 *World Evangelization*, publication of the Lausanne Committee for World Evangelization, Vol 13 No 48, Sept–Oct 1987
2 *Management Today*, March 1988, Page 117
3 *Christian History* journal, Issue 16, Pages 2 and 7
4 John Haggai, *Lead On!*, Word, Waco, Texas, 1986, Page 11
5 Roland Gribben, Business Editor, *Daily Telegraph*, July 21st, 1988
6 Matthew 23:23, 24:2, 24:3, 24:23, 24:27 (RSV)
7 Report in *Daily Telegraph*, July 12th, 1988
8 BBC Television Report of Conference, June 11th, 1988
9 Report in *Daily Telegraph*, August 8th, 1988
10 *Decision* magazine, April 1988
11 Report in *USA Today*, August 17th, 1988
12 *Daily Telegraph* leader, April 1st, 1986
13 Robert Schuller, *Your Church has a Fantastic Future*, Regal, 1986
14 Adminisheet 8, from Administry, April 1987
15 Elisabeth Eliot, *Amy Carmichael*, MARC, 1988, Page 358
16 Ray Anderson, *Minding God's Business*, Grand Rapids, Michigan, Eerdmans, 1986
17 *Tyne and Wear Christian Directory*, edited David Longley & Mervyn Spearing, MARC Europe, 1986
18 Dr David Cormack, *Seconds Away!*, MARC Europe, 1985
19 Ed Dayton and Ted Engstrom, *Strategy for Leadership*, MARC Europe, 1985
20 Richard Worthing-Davies, Executive Director, personal communication, December 15th, 1987
21 Quoted in *International Management*, July/August 1988: my italics
22 Peter Brierley, *Mission to London Part II: Who went forward?*, MARC Europe, 1985
23 *Redemption* magazine, September 1988, Page 9

24 Article in *Daily Telegraph*, August 17th, 1988
25 Buck Rogers, *The IBM Way*, Guild Publishing, 1986, Page 117
26 Reginald Maudling, *Observer*, 'Sayings of 1964', December 27th, 1964
27 Edward Phelps, American lawyer, quoted in *Business Quotations*
28 Tom Sine, *Why Settle for More and Miss the Best?*, Milton Keynes, Word Publishing, 1987, Page 153

Chapter 2

1 Alan R. Tippett, *Church Growth and the Word of God*, Grand Rapids, Michigan, Eerdmans, 1970
2 Oliver Wendell Holmes, Sr, *The Poet at the Breakfast Table*
3 Robert Waterman, *The Renewal Factor*, London, Bantam, 1988, Page 6
4 J. Oswald Saunders, 'Am I Ready?', *Decision* magazine, September 1988
5 *Dictionary of the Pentecostal and Charismatic Movements*, edited by Stanley M. Burgess and Gary B. McGee, Zondervan Publishing House, 1988, Article by Prof C. Peter Wagner
6 Peter Wagner, *Spiritual Power and Church Growth*, Altamonte Springs, Strang, 1986
7 Dean Drayton, *God's New Age*, Board of Mission, New South Wales Synod, Uniting Church in Australia, 1985
8 Revd Dr David Barrett, *World Christian Encyclopaedia*, Oxford University Press, 1982
9 Revd Dr Donald English, *Methodist Recorder*, January 1985
10 Reginald Bibby, *Fragmented Gods*, Toronto, Irwin Publishing, 1987, Page 232
11 *Political, Social and Economic Review*, NOP, Number 48, June 1984, Page 29
12 *Above Bar Church*, Church Attendance Survey Report, MARC Europe, 1987
13 *Gold Hill Baptist Church*, Education Survey, 1987
14 *UK Christian Handbook*, 1989/90 Edition, MARC Europe, 1988, Table 13
15 *OPCS Monitor*, FM2 87/1, 87/2, Office of Population Censuses and Surveys, October 1987
16 Quoted in *LandMARC*, Easter 1988, from a Conference on Reaching the Nation's Children conducted by the Evangelical Alliance, January 1988

17 Home Office figures quoted in *Statistical News*, HMSO, August 1987
18 *Ibid*
19 *Op cit* (item 16)
20 Ken Morgan, *Redemption*, October 1988, Page 10
21 Chris DeWet, *Redemption*, October 1988, Page 13
22 David Bridge, *The Missionary Shape of the Congregation*, Methodist Churches, Home Mission Division, 1988
23 *English Life Tables*, Office of Population Censuses and Surveys, as reproduced in *LandMARC*, High Summer, 1987
24 *Background to the Task*, Scripture Union, 1968
25 All the percentages are quoted from answers given in the Leeds Common Religion Project, Dr Robert Towler. See questions numbered 159, 339, 163, 164, 200, 202, 204, 205, 207 and 210 respectively
26 Leslie Francis, *Youth in Transit*, Gower Press, 1982, Page 25 and *Experience of Adulthood*, Gower Press, 1982, Page 24
27 David Lyon, *Third Way*, July/August 1984
28 Melanie Cottrell, *Invisible Religion & the Middle Class*, unpublished paper, 1979
29 Os Guinness, *The Gravedigger File*, Hodder & Stoughton, 1983, Page 147f
30 Thomas Luckmann, *The Invisible Religion*, London, Collier-Macmillan, 1967
31 *Op cit* (item 28)
32 H. R. Snyder, *Foresight*, Nelson, 1986, Pages 115–16
33 Essay 8 on Decline of Religion (1946) in *Undeceptions*, Bless, 1971, Pages 178–9
34 Professor J. Russell Hale, *The Unchurched*, New York, Harper & Row, 1977
35 *Recent Trends in Church Membership and Participation*, David A. Roozen and Jackson W. Carroll, *c* 1980
36 Alan Flavelle, 'The Church Today and Tomorrow,' *Journal of the Irish Christian Study Centre*, Vol 2, 1984, Page 27
37 Ed Dayton, *Whatever Happened to Commitment?*, Zondervan, 1984, Page 20
38 Revd Edward Bailey, unpublished text, Page 154
39 Dr Steve Bruce, Conservative Protestantism in the UK, *Sociological Review*, August 1983
40 Professor David Martin, *Prospects for the Eighties Vol I*, Bible Society, 1980
41 *British Social Attitudes: The 1984 Report*, edited by Roger Jowell and Colin Airey, SCPR, Gower, 1984

42 The Methodist Study referred to in item 22 above suggests church size may be an insignificant factor in church growth.

43 See also the essay by Revd Dr Roy Pointer in *Prospects for the Eighties Vol II*, Bible Society and MARC Europe, 1983

44 *Clergy Numbers: Projection to 2007*, General Synod (Misc) 270, Church of England, June 1987, and *The Ordained Ministry: Numbers, Cost and Deployment*, Green Discussion Paper, Ministry Co-ordinating Group, General Synod, November 1988

45 *Church Times*, August 26th, 1988

46 *Op cit* (item 14) Table 16 for Anglicans, and *op cit* (item 22) Page 20 for Methodists

47 *The Tablet*, August 30th, 1986

48 *Personnel Survey*, Evangelical Missionary Alliance, 1986

49 Habakkuk 2:2 (RSV)

Chapter 3

1 William Manchester, *The Caged Lion*, London, Michael Joseph, 1988, Page 681

2 Genesis 46:2, 1 Samuel 3:11, Daniel 2:3, 1 Chronicles 17:15, 1 Kings 11:29–39, 2 Chronicles 26:5 respectively

3 Luke 1:22, Acts 9:10, 12, 10:3, 17, 16:9, 18:9, Revelation 9:17 and 2 Corinthians 12:2 (NIV) respectively

4 Genesis 15:2, 46:2, 1 Samuel 3:10, Daniel 10:17 (NIV), Luke 1:18, Acts 9:13, 10:4, 10:14 and Revelation 7:14 respectively

5 Daniel 8:15 (NIV), Matthew 17:9 (NIV), Revelation 9:17 (NIV) respectively

6 Ezekiel 8:10, Daniel 7:8, 1 Chronicles 17, 2 Samuel 7, Acts 10:12 and Revelation 10:4 respectively

7 Ezekiel 8:11; 40–48, Daniel 2:14, 19 and 8:27 respectively

8 Ezekiel 1:4, 1:20, 2:2, 3:3, 8:3 (NIV) and 11:24 (NIV) respectively

9 Matthew 17, Acts 9:8, 10:10–16, Luke 1:22, Isaiah 6:7, Ezekiel 2:2, Daniel 8:18, 10:11, 10:10, Ezekiel 8:8, 11:13, 3:3 and Revelation 10:9 respectively

10 Genesis 15:1, 4; 1 Samuel 3:8, 3:1, Ezekiel 1:3, 11:14, 1 Chronicles 17:3, Isaiah 21:6, Matthew 17:5 and Acts 18:9 respectively

11 Ezekiel 3:12, 8:3, 11:1, 24, 43:5 for example, Ezekiel 11:5, Joel 2:28 and Acts 10:19 respectively (NIV)

12 Genesis 46:2, Daniel 7:1, 4:13, 1 Samuel 3:3, 1 Chronicles 17:3, Acts 16:9 and 18:9 respectively

13 Ezekiel 1:1, Daniel 10:4, Acts 10:30, 10:9, 26:13–19, Luke 24:23
14 Acts 10:17, 11:11, 9:10, 12, 2 Samuel 7:17, 1 Chronicles 17:15, Habakkuk 2:1 and Isaiah 6:11 respectively
15 Daniel 2:18–19, 10:12, 1 Samuel 3:1 (NIV), Amos 7:14 (NIV), Luke 1:12 and Acts 10:4 respectively
16 2 Corinthians 12:2, 4 (NIV), Revelation 4:1 and 2 Corinthians 12:3 respectively
17 Isaiah 1:1, 2 Chronicles 32:32, Daniel 2:19, and 2:28 respectively
18 1 Chronicles 9:29 and 1 Chronicles 17:15
19 Hosea 12:10, Obadiah 1, Nahum 1:1, Daniel 4:9, and Numbers 12:6, 8 (RSV) respectively
20 Numbers 24:16 and Acts 10:14 (italics mine), respectively
21 Revelation 9:17, 1:3 and 22:10 respectively
22 Lamentations 2:9 and Ezekiel 2:5
23 See for example the interview with Terry Fulham, in *Leadership* magazine, Winter 1984, Volume V, Number 1, Page 21
24 Zechariah 13:2 and 4 (NIV)
25 Ezekiel 12:24, 13:6, 7, 8, 9, 16, 23, then 2, 3 and 4 respectively
26 *The Lion Handbook to the Bible*, Lion, 1973
27 *Matthew Henry's Commentary on the whole Bible*, Marshall, Morgan and Scott, 1960
28 Ezekiel 21:29, 22:28, Jeremiah 14:14 and 23:16
29 Tom Sine, *The Mustard Seed Conspiracy*, MARC Europe, 1984
30 Daniel 7:28, 8:26 and 12:4, Revelation 10:4, Habakkuk 2:3 and Isaiah 6:10 respectively
31 Genesis 15:2, Acts 16:10 and 18:10 respectively
32 Isaiah 1:1 and 6:9, italics mine
33 Ezekiel 8 and 11, Daniel 4:19, 8:17, 10:14 and 8:27 respectively
34 1 Chronicles 17, 1 Samuel 3, Acts 9 and Acts 10 respectively
35 Genesis 16:3, 16; 47:9
36 Jamieson, Fausset and Brown, *Commentary on the whole Bible*, Oliphant, 1961
37 Acts 2:16, 36 and 38; italics mine
38 Isaiah 1:1, 6:12, Ezekiel 8:12, Acts 10:35, 16:7 and Matthew 17:5 respectively
39 Genesis 5:4, 24:7, 15:13, 1 Samuel 2:17, 2:31, 3:11–12, Ezekiel 12:27, 28, 23, 26:17, Habakkuk 2:3, Daniel 7:18 and Revelation 5:10 respectively
40 1 Chronicles 17:15, Acts 16:10, 18:11, 26:19, Luke 1:13, Acts 10:5, Ezekiel 2:4, 11:4 and Romans 8:26, 27 respectively
41 Genesis 46:2, Acts 18:10, Ezekiel 40:4, 43:7, 1 Chronicles 17:11, 12 and 2 Corinthians 12:7 respectively

42 Luke 1:13, Acts 10:4, Daniel 9:20, 22, 23 and John 16:24 respectively
43 Job 42:3, 5; italics mine
44 Habakkuk 2:2 (RSV), Acts 10:17, 20, 23, 2 Corinthians 12:2 and Deuteronomy 13:1–3 respectively
45 2 Samuel 12:20, 7:2, 1 Chronicles 16:8, 9, 10, 25, Daniel 2:20 and Acts 11:18 respectively
46 Genesis 46:3, 5, 1 Chronicles 17:23, Acts 9:17, 10:8, 11:12, 16:10 and 26:19 respectively
47 Genesis 15:6 and 1 Samuel 3:18
48 Ezekiel 11:24, 25, Daniel 2:28 and 4:32 respectively
49 Acts 11:13, 14, 16:10, 18:10 and 26:20 respectively
50 1 Samuel 3:15, Job 4:13, 7:14, 33:16, Daniel 4:19, Matthew 17:6, Luke 1:12 and 24:5, 23 respectively
51 Daniel 4:19, 7:15, 28, 10:8, 16, 7, Ezekiel 3:15 Amplified Version, and Isaiah 21:4 respectively
52 Isaiah 21:2, 3, Daniel 8:27, Job 4:14, Daniel 10:7 and Acts 9:7 respectively
53 Daniel 9:23, 10:12 and 12:8, Acts 10:17, 19 and 1 Corinthians 14:27 respectively
54 Isaiah 21:2 probably refers to Babylon
55 Luke 24:23, Acts 10:3, Luke 1:22, Daniel 8:16, and Revelation 7:13 respectively

Chapter 4

1 Personal letter from Revd D. G. Douglas, Overcoming Faith Miracle Ministries, 1988
2 *Prophecy Today*, Vol 3, No 5, Sept/Oct 1987
3 Gordon Heald and Robert Wybrow, *The Gallup Survey of Britain*, Croom Helm, Beckenham, 1986, Ch 23 Daydreams
4 The full story is told by Rosalind Allan in *Out of the Ark*, Hodder & Stoughton, 1988
5 John Naisbitt, *Re-inventing the Corporation*, London, Guild Publishing, 1985, Page 21.
6 H. Ross Perot (founder of Electronic Data Systems) quoted in Robert Waterman's *The Renewal Factor*, London, Bantam, 1988, Page 43
7 *Moneycare*, July/August 1987, Sue Birley on Page 11
8 R. Keith Parks, *World in View*, Global Evangelization Movement, AD 2000 Series, Foreign Mission Board, Southern Baptist Convention, New Hope, Alabama, 1987
9 *The Sojourners* magazine August/September 1986

10 Ray Bakke, *The Urban Christian*, MARC Europe, 1987
11 Professor Max De Pree, *Leadership is an Art*, Michigan State University Press, 1987
12 C. Peter Wagner, *Your Spiritual Gifts can help your Church Grow*, MARC Europe, 1985
13 Bernard Haldane, *How to make a habit of success*, Warner, 1975; later editions are entitled *Career Satisfaction and Success*
14 Quoted from *The Renewal Factor* (*Op cit*, item 6), Page 127
15 William Manchester, *The Caged Lion*, London, Michael Joseph, 1988, Page 427
16 *Op cit* (Item 6) Page 96
17 Michael Bunker, *The Church on the Hill*, MARC, 1988
18 Gavin Reid, *Hope for the Church of England*, Kingsway, July 1986
19 *Redemption* magazine, January 1987, Page 9
20 From the catalogue description of George Melby's biography, published by Thames and Hudson, 1987
21 *USA Today*, August 12th, 1988
22 Quoted in *Grapevine*, the Christian Newsletter for the Plymouth area, Jan/Feb 1989, Page 5
23 *Op cit* (Item 22) Page 4
24 Adapted from *Decision* magazine, July/August 1987
25 Advertisement in *Daily Telegraph*, March 16th, 1989
26 *Decision* magazine, October 1988, Page 23
27 *Decision* magazine, July/August 1987, article by Janet Wise, Page 35
28 Peter Block, *The Empowered Manager*, London, Jossey-Bass Publishers, 1987, Pages 102, 115.

Chapter 5

1 Lord Cockfield, former EEC Internal Market Commissioner, speaking to the Greek Management Association in Athens, and reported in *International Management*, March 1989, Page 11
2 Based closely on material in *Vision Building and Strategic Planning*, a MARC Europe Seminar hand-out originally written by Dr David Cormack
3 *Ibid*
4 *Ibid*
5 Revd Stephen Gaukroger, *Leadership Today*, October 1987, Page 31

6 *Leadership*, Fall 1985
7 Max De Pree, *Leadership is an Art*, Michigan State University Press, 1987, Page 127
8 Tom Sine, *The Mustard Seed Conspiracy*, MARC Europe, 1985
9 *AIM International* magazine, First Issue 1988, Pages 3, 4

Chapter 6

1 British Institute of Management, *Management News*, Autumn 1988
2 John Naisbitt and Patricia Abundene, *Re-inventing the Corporation*, London, Guild Publishing, 1985, Page 28
3 From presentation at a church weekend in November 1986 for Christ Church, Bromley
4 G. J. Pearson, *The Strategic Discount*, John Wiley & Sons, 1983
5 Robert Waterman, *The Renewal Factor*, London, Bantam, 1988, Page 66
6 *Ibid*, Pages 12–13
7 *The Frontiersman* newsletter, 1988, Page 6
8 Lee Iacocca, *Talking Straight*, Sidgwick and Jackson, 1988
9 See also Mrs Elizabeth Gibson, *House Style Notes*, MARC Monograph No 7, 1986, on which some of this text is based
10 John Naisbitt, *Megatrends*, MacDonald, 1984, Page 72

Chapter 7

1 Some of the early material in this chapter is taken from Ron Steele, *Destined to Win*, Conquest RSA, 1986

INDEX

Abortions, 47, 154
Above Bar Church, 24, 163
Abram, 19, 81, 83, 86, 87, 88, 89, 94, 95, 97, 101, 120, 127, 130, 132
Addicott, Ernie, 155f
Affiliation and risk, 187
Africa Inland Mission, 159, 167
African/West Indian churches, 50, 69
Age of church-goers, 53, 154
Age of ministers, 69
All Souls Church, 16
Allan, Rosalind, 111
Amos, prophet, 89, 104, 110
Analogy, 152
Ananias, 83, 84, 89, 101
Anderson, Ray, 20
Anglican(s), 21, 39, 49, 51, 64, 68, 69, 70, 139, 141, 142, 149, 159, 194, 195
Anglo-Catholics, 50
Arab-Israeli war, 155
Arbuckle, Gerald, 69
Assimilating the vision, 173
Aswan Dam, 180
Attendance, church, 39, 49, 51, 53, 154

Bailey, Dr Edward, 61, 62
Baker, Kenneth, 18
Bakke, Ray, 114, 147
Balaam, 91
Baptist(s), 40, 49, 51, 68, 69, 137, 138, 141, 158, 194
Barrett, Dr David, 45, 65, 66

Baughen, Bishop, 19
Beasley-Murray, Dr Paul, 146
Becoming, 122
Belief and change, 184
Benton, Colin, 126
Bewes, Richard, 16
Bible Society, 21, 27
Blessing, Buck, 107
Block, Peter, 132
Bonkke, Reinhard, 198
Bracknell Baptist Church, 42, 185, 194
Brandhall Church, 24, 159
Brethren, Christian, 22, 71
Bridge, David, 51
Bridge, Donald, 99
British Institute of Management, 21
British Social Attitudes, 64
Browning, Bishop, 18
Bruce, Steve, 64
Brunel, Isambard, 13
Bunker, Michael, 126
Bunting, Ian, 173

Cambodia, 11
Campolo, Tony, 122
Campus Crusade for Christ, 24
Canon Inc, 30
Canterbury, Archbishop of, 30
Carey, William, 111
Carmichael, Amy, 20
Carnegie, Dale, 193
Carroll, Lewis, 32
Catholic(s), 21, 39, 40, 49, 50, 51, 64, 68, 69, 78

Chacour, Father Elias, 14
Challenge of vision, 108, 181
Change and
    education, 46
    morality, 47
    religion, 47
    society, 48
    technology, 46
    vision, 36, 163, 180f
Charismatics, 43
Chesterton, G. K., 186
China Inland Mission, 34, 128,
    176
Cho, Dr Paul Yonggi, 42, 110, 173
Christ Church, Bromley, 139, 195
Christ Church, Gateshead, 21
Christian Aid, 21
Christian and Missionary
    Alliance, 159
Chrysler Motor Corp, 159
Church Army, 159
Church growth, 43
Church of Scotland, 40
Church Pastoral-Aid Society, 159
Churchill, Sir Winston, 81, 125, 126
City Technology Colleges, 36
Cleaver, Eldridge, 164
Cockfield, Lord, 135
Columbus, Christopher, 34
Commitment, loss of, 57
Communicating the vision, 163,
    178, 188f, 193, 199
Community, Christian, 63
Complacency, 182
Confidence, loss of, 182
Consequences of vision, 32
Constraints, too many, 183
Context of vision, 39
Cormack, Dr David, 5, 25, 111,
    162, 169, 183
Cornelius, 84, 88, 89, 98, 101, 102
Corporate vision, 135f
Cosby, Gordon, 113
Cottrell, Melanie, 56, 61
Creation, 20
Crime numbers, 48
Crispness of vision, 124, 158

Crusaders, 21, 155f
Crystal, John, 107
Culture, 45, 177
Currie, H. M., 84

Daniel, prophet, 84, 86, 87, 88,
    89, 91, 94, 95, 98, 99, 102, 103,
    185, 200
Darnall, Jean, 127
Darwin, Charles, 55
Data collection, 39
David, King, 19, 20, 40, 83, 86,
    95, 98, 100, 101, 122, 185
Dayton, Ed, 25, 61, 180
De Pree, Max, 115
Definition of vision, 20, 22
Determination, 131
Diagrams, 191
Discontinuity, 127, 166
Disease, 152
Disraeli, Benjamin, 131
Dissatisfaction, 37, 161, 183, 193
Distractions, 129
Divorces, 47
Dobson, James, 110, 124
Dohnavur Fellowship, 20
Douglas, Peter, 110
Doyle, Arthur Conan, 113
Dreams, 34, 84f, 111
Dreams are not Enough, 85
Drive of vision, 15
Drucker, Peter, 25
Drug use, 48
Dunnett, Bob, 34

Ebenezer Church, 22
Education, 18, 36, 46
Edwardes, Sir Michael, 37
Egyptians, 184
Einstein, Albert, 16
Elderly church-goers, 52
Electoral Roll, 39
Elliot, Jim, 108
Elliott, J. H., 181
Emerson, Ralph Waldo, 31
Empire, British, 152
Empire, Roman, 27

Encouragement, 99, 132
Endorsement of vision, 166
Energy of vision, 30
England, Edward, 132
English, Rev Dr Donald, 45
Engstrom, Dr Ted, 25, 180
Environment, 178
Esteem and risk, 188
Ethnic churches, 40, 71
Evangelism, 163, 193
Excellence in ministry, 200
Excitement and vision, 131
Experience, 113
Ezekiel, prophet, 86, 87, 88, 90,
    92, 94, 97, 98, 102, 103, 104,
    200

Faith and vision, 33, 82, 126
Faith in the City, 138
Farnborough Hospital, 178
Fear, 182
Finance received, 71
First steps and change, 184
Flavelle, Alan, 61
Fleming, Alexander, 130
Footprinting, 151f, 157
Fragmentation of churches, 62
Frightened by vision, 103
Functions of a church, 146
Future, facing the, 18, 173

Gairdner Ministries, 137, 159 (as
    People International)
Gallup, George Jnr, 56
Gateshead, 21
Gaukroger, Stephen, 163
Generation change, 64
Gibbs, Prof Eddie, 140
Gide, André, 33
Gifts, 114f
Glasgow Archdiocese, 189
Goals, 25, 26, 193, 199
God, belief in, 58
God's will, word and work, 20, 26
Gorbachev, Mikhail, 17
Gore, Bill, 131

Graham, Dr Billy, 13, 18, 68, 120,
    131, 153, 154
Grant, Bill, 20
Graphs, 192
Greenslade, Philip, 108
Guidance, 98, 108
Guinness, Os, 56

Habakkuk, prophet, 89, 100
Haggai, John, 30, 31
Haggai, prophet, 37, 161
Haldane, Bernard, 117
Hale, Prof, 58
Hammarskjöld, Dag, 193
Hardin, Garrett, 180
Harper, Michael, 30
Hedonists, 59
Heraclitus, 184
Holmes, Prof Oliver, 42
Holmes, Peter, 5
Holmes, Sherlock, 113
Holy Trinity, Leicester, 195
Hope and vision, 131
Hosea, prophet, 91
House Churches, 50, 52, 67, 69,
    71, 154, 163
Houston, Rev Tom, 43, 44
Humility of vision, 31, 121, 125

Iacocca, Lee, 14, 37, 186
IBM, 36
Identifying vision, 120
Illegitimacy, 48
Importance, 104, 160
Impossible, 32, 127
Income of para-church agencies,
    71f
Independent churches, 50, 51
Indicators, 153
Influences, 82
Information, value of, 41, 112
Invisible, 20
Irreversible, 90
Irvine, Graeme, 186
Irwin, James, 11
Isaiah, prophet, 87, 89, 90, 103,
    104

Isolation, 182

Jacob, patriarch, 83, 84, 90, 95, 97, 101, 132
Jehovah's Witnesses, 47, 64
Jesus, Messiah, 17, 28, 55, 84, 99, 122, 153
Job, servant, 17, 99, 103
Joel, prophet, 84, 88, 96
John, apostle, 83, 84, 86, 92
Joseph, Prime Minister, 35, 127, 183, 200
Joseph, Sir Keith, 18
Jowell, Henry, 112
Jubliee Centre, 25

King, Martin Luther, 34, 35, 133
Kinnock, Neil, 18
Knowledge, 179
Knox, John Church, 22
Korean Christians, 43

Laban household, 120
Lausanne Committee, 44
Lausanne Congress, 13
Leader's vision, 164
Learning, 129
Leech, William, 125
Leeds Project, 64
Legacy income, 53, 154
Lewis, C. S., 57, 132
Lewis, Raymond, 173
Life after death, 55
Livingstone, David, 123
Longfellow, 125
Los Angeles headmistress, 124
Luckmann, 56
Luther, Martin, 17
Lyon, David, 55

McCauley, Ray, 197f
McGavran, Prof Donald, 130
Maguire, Robert, 194
Manchester Guardian, 125
MARC Europe, 22, 23, 25, 107, 135, 167, 183
Martin, Prof David, 64

Mary, mother of Jesus, 121
Maslow hierarchy, 186f
Matthew, apostle, 122
Maudling, Reginald, 37
Mawhinney, Brian, 29
Membership, church, change, 49, 154
Membership, church, giving, 74
Messiah, 132
Methodist(s), 21, 39, 49, 51, 68, 69, 70
Milosz, Czeslaw, 127
Ministers, 68, 143, 144
Mission, 21, 26
Mission England, 45, 153
Mission to London, 33, 45, 153
Missionaries, 76f, 143, 144, 145, 154, 177
Models of churches, 140, 192
Morgan, Campbell, 132
Mormons, 47, 64
Morris, Rev Colin, 46
Moses, leader, 16, 19, 20, 28, 84, 91, 100, 104, 183, 184
Mothers' Union, 21, 24
Motivation, 163, 193
Mott, Dr John, 25
Motto, 158
Müller, George, 34
Murphy, Terry, 32
Muslims, 47, 137, 186

Nahum, prophet, 91
Nain, widow of, 166
Naisbitt, John, 29, 36, 107, 112, 173, 191
Nathan, prophet, 83, 87, 88, 89, 90
Nebuchadnezzar, King, 83, 88, 91, 200
Negative reactions to vision, 102, 114
Nehemiah, cup bearer, 27, 177
New Churches, *see under* House Churches
New Zealand, 174
Newcastle, 22
Noah, builder, 104

Nominal Christianity, 54
Numbers, simple, 190f

Obadiah, prophet, 91
Obedience, 101, 132
Objectives, 178
Opposition and vision, 35
Orthodox churches, 49, 50, 51, 68
Overseas Missionary Fellowship, 128, 159, 176
Oxfam, 21

Palau, Luis, 33, 111
Para-church agencies, 43, 53, 71f
Parker, Sir Peter, 131
Paul, apostle, 20, 27, 31, 83, 87, 90, 94, 95, 96, 97, 98, 100, 101, 102, 129, 132, 175
Pearson, G. J., 178
Pentecost, Ed, 146
Pentecostals, 43, 50, 52, 69, 71
People, 179, 181
People International, 159
Peter, Apostle, 84, 86, 87, 88, 89, 90, 92, 95, 96, 97, 100, 101, 103, 132, 185
Pictures, 192
Piecharts, 192
Pitlochry Baptist Church, 158
Planning, 23, 25, 26, 27, 123, 135, 148, 179, 199
Plato, 113
Poland, 127
Population, 44, 154
Portman, Sister L., 178
Praise, 100
Prayer and vision, 99, 110, 171, 173
Presbyterian(s), 49, 51, 68, 69, 70
Principles, guiding, 26
Priorities, 25, 26, 159
Privatisation of religion, 56
Proclamation and vision, 102
Prophets and visions, 90
Prospects, surveys, 51, 52, 66
Purpose, 20, 26
Pursuing the vision, 127
Puttnam, David, 29

Pyne, Cliff, 195

Quayle, Dan, 18

Radio One, 47
Realism, 29
Reddaway, Rev David, 175
Reid, Rev Gavin, 126
Religion, change and, 47
Responsibilities, 178
Revelation, 105, 162
Review, 26, 199
Risk of vision, 33, 185f
Rogers, Jenny, 7
Roman Catholic, see under Catholic
Roozen and Carroll, 61
Rowan, Roy, 124
Running with the vision, 197f

Safety and risk, 188
St Agnes Church, 21
St Andrew Diocese, 189
St Chad's Church, Derby, 194
St Paul's Cathedral, 42, 107
Salesian Sisters, 22, 23, 157
Salvation Army, 22, 41, 67
Samson, strongman, 19
Samuel, judge, 83, 84, 87, 88, 89, 95, 96, 101, 103, 122
Scenario thinking, 155
Schuller, Robert, 19, 163, 193
Scriptures, 16, 20, 81f, 87, 105, 109, 162
Self-interest, 182
Service and risk, 188
Sex Discrimination Act, 113
Sex of church-goers, 53
Sheehan, George, 125
Shell International, 155
Shirley, Steve, 131
Sider, Ron, 44
Sine, Tom, 37, 93, 165
Singaporean Christians, 43
Size of church, 66
Skills, 117f
Smoking and children, 48

Social scene, 156
Sölle, Dorothy, 19
South Africa, 197
Southampton, 24
Southeast Asian Outreach, 12, 23
Spirit, Holy, 20, 27
Stakeholders, 142, 143
Statistics
　church, 39
　value of, 41
Stimulation of vision, 14
Stott, Rev Dr John, 200
Strategy, 26, 75, 126, 133, 178
Stress on ministers, 70
Structure for vision, 176
Studd, C. T., 109
Sunday, Billy, 54
Sunday School, 47, 140, 143, 144
Sung, John, 15
Surveys, 138
Survival and risk, 186
Swift, Jonathan, 20

Taing, Major Chirrac, 11
Taylor, Cyril, 36
Taylor, Hudson, 34, 42, 176
Taylor, James III, 176
Technology, changing, 46
Telford, 13
Thatcher, Margaret, 17
Third World Missions, 43
Thrusts, 24, 26, 167, 169, 189
Tidball, Rev Dr Derek, 127
Timmins, Mark, 12
Titanic, 193
Townsend, Anne, 107
Tradition, 181
Training, 70, 75, 130
Transformation of vision, 14
Trans-World Airlines, 159
Trends, 139
Trust, 101
Tunstall, Bishop, 15
Turner, 112
Tyndale, William, 15
Tyneside, 21, 22
Tysoe, James, 5

UCCF, 174
UK Christian Handbook, 44, 49,
　51, 68, 71, 77, 191
Unchurched, The, 58·
Understanding, 100
United Reformed Church, 22
Urbanisation, 44
Urgency, 160

Values, 177
Violence, 48
Virginity, 48
Vision
　assimilating the, 173
　beyond oneself, 30
　building a, 109
　challenging, 108
　change, and, 36, 180f, 183
　clear, 29
　communicating the, 188f, 199
　consequences of, 32
　contemporary, 17
　context of, 39f
　corporate, 135f
　crispness of, 124
　definition of, 22
　detailed, 86
　dissatisfaction, and, 37
　dreams, and, 34, 84f, 111
　drive, 15
　effect of, 100
　encouragement, and, 99, 132
　energising, 30
　enlarge understanding, 97
　essential, 15
　excitement, and, 131
　experience, and, 113
　external stimuli, and, 86
　faith, and, 33, 82, 126
　future, face the, 18, 97
　gifts, and, 114
　God, and, 83
　guidance, and, 98, 108
　helps others, 108
　hope, and, 131
　humbling, 31
　identifying the, 120

importance of, 104
information, and, 112
irreversible, 90
key people, given to, 82
leader of the, 164
leadership, and the, 165
making it work, 163
meaning of the word, 85
need for, 13
obedience, and, 101, 132
opposition, and, 35
personal, 28
planning, and, 166
praise, and, 100
prayer, and, 99, 110, 171, 173
proclamation, and, 102
prophetic nature of, 90
pursuing the, 127
realistic, 29
risk and, 33, 185f
running with the, 197f
Scriptures, and the, 16, 20, 81f, 87, 109
shareable, 29
skills, and, 117
stimulation of, 14
strategic, 133
structure for, 176
transformation by, 14, 90
trust, and, 101
understanding, and, 97, 100

women, and, 83, 88
Workshop, 136, 165
Visuals, simple, 191

Wagner, Prof Peter, 43, 115
Wałesa, Lech, 121
War, 152, 154, 155
Watson, David, 123
Watson, Thomas J., 36
Wavell, Lord, 185
Weariness and change, 182
Webber, Max, 56
Whitburn Methodist Church, 21
Wilson, Scottie, 127
Wilson, Tom, 166
Wimber, John, 109
Winter, Ralph, 32
Women and vision, 83, 88
Words, simple, 188
World Christian Encyclopaedia, 45, 65
World Vision, 24, 43, 177, 186
Worldwide Evangelical Fellowship, 44

YMCA survey, 55
Young men, 95

Zechariah, prophet, 83, 84, 87, 88, 89, 90, 98, 99, 103
Zwemer, Dr Samuel, 186

SCRIPTURE INDEX

This index excludes the many Scriptural references used in Chapter 3, which are identified, in the Notes for that Chapter, on Page 206.

Genesis 50:20, 127
Exodus 12:6, 184
Numbers 12:6, 84
  24:4, 16, 84
1 Chronicles 21, 40
2 Chronicles 26:5, 91
  34, 112
Job 4:13, 85
  7:14, 85
  20:8, 85
  33:15, 85
  42:3, 31
Psalm 89:19, 104
  115:1, 125
  119:33, 16
Proverbs 3:5,6, 122
  29:18, 15, 105, 196
Ecclesiastes 11:1, 132
Isaiah 6, 104
  22:1,5, 104
  28:7, 93
  29:7, 85
  29:9–11, 94
Jeremiah, 23:16, 92
Ezekiel, 7:13, 90
  7:26, 91
  10:22, 200
Daniel 1:17, 85

Joel 2:28, 84, 96
Amos 5:24, 44
  7:1–9, 111
Micah 3:5,6, 92
Habakkuk 2:3, 122
Haggai 1:6,8, 161
  2:5,6,9,22, 161

Matthew 7:20, 108
  17:20, 34
Luke 14:28, 170
  21:29,30, 154
John 3:16, 30, 174
Acts 1:7, 155
Romans 8:21, 131
1 Corinthians 13:11, 188
  14:40, 200
  15:43,44, 132
  15:52, 132
2 Corinthians 4:18, 132
  12:2,4, 90
Ephesians 1:4, 31
  2:10, 31
  3:11, 31
  3:20, 131
Hebrews 11:1, 34
  11:27, 16

CHRISTIAN RESEARCH ASSOCIATION

The vision of the Christian Research Association (CRA) is that by the year 2000, the use of relevant research by Christian leaders in strategic planning will be commonplace. *Reaching and Keeping Teenagers* is one such example.

The CRA publishes the *UK Christian Handbook* (UKCH) every two years. It is a mine of information on British Christianity, a one-volume reference library giving 17 pieces of information for over 5,000 organisation in the United Kingdom. It is not just bought in Britain. Ted Limpio, of Sepal in Brazil, wrote, "I couldn't help but be impressed by the quality and thoroughness of your work."

Corporate members of the CRA get a hardback copy of the UKCH *free*, and individual members are able to buy it at a substantial discount. Members also get the information bulletin, *Quadrant*, five times a year, are able to access the CRA Resources Library gratis, and are entitled to discounts on research work and training seminars.

Ask for more details of the CRA **today** by writing to the Christian Research Association, Vision Building, 4 Footscray Road, Eltham, London SE9 2TZ, or phone us on 081-294-1989. We look forward to hearing from you.